The Moody Legacy

An Illustrated History

1827-2005

This book is sold subject to the condition that it shall not, by way of trade or otherwise, be lent, re-sold, hired out, or otherwise circulated without the publisher's prior consent in any form of binding or cover other than that in which it is published and without a similar condition including this condition being imposed on the subsequent publisher.

The moral right of David Moody has been asserted.

First published in Great Britain in 2008 by Warsash Publishing, 6 Dibles Road, Warsash, SO31 9HZ

ISBN: 9780948646850

Designed & printed by Colourspeed, Fareham.

The Moody Legacy

An Illustrated History

1827-2005

by David Moody

Warsash Publishing

Dedication

I would like to dedicate this work to my parents, Patricia and Gordon Moody. Their life experiences such as living through the hardship of the Second World War and the post war recovery years taught them that when opportunities arose, you should try to make things happen rather than to expect things to come to you. My father believed that to stand still was never an option where the business was concerned. This philosophy rubbed off on me. The world doesn't owe you a living.

Finally, my thanks to my wife, Trish, for the endless hours she has spent with me putting this project together. Without her input and support things would not have happened!

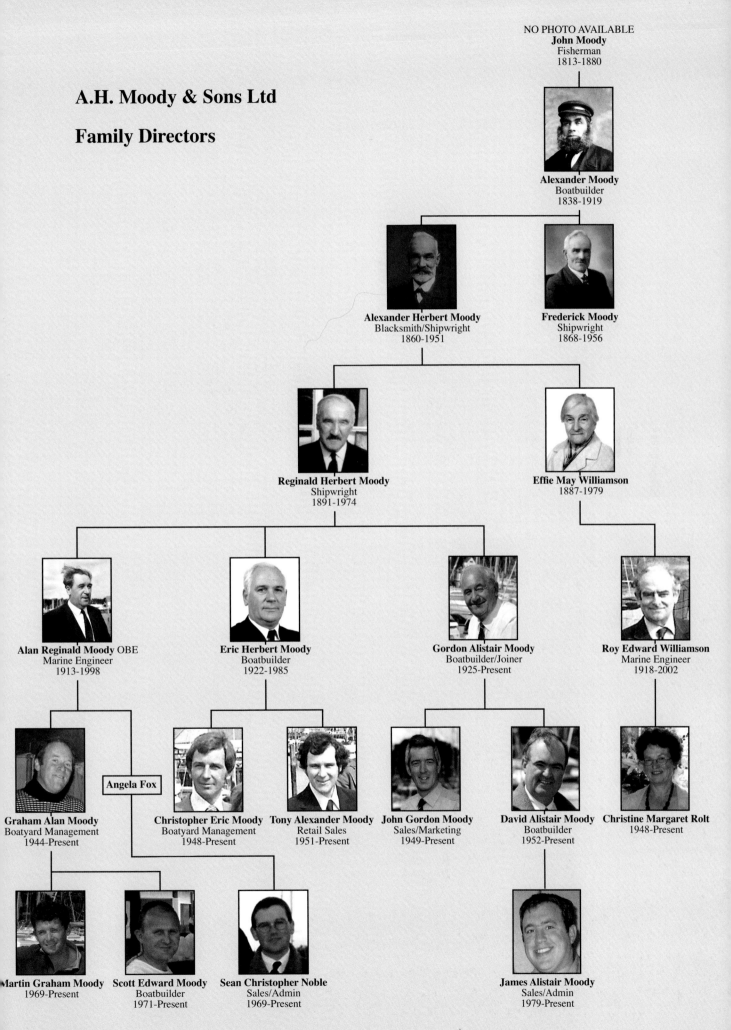

Acknowledgements

My special thanks to:

Mrs Joan Jardine-Brown: Joan's advice and memories as daughter of designer T. Harrison-Butler has been invaluable. She generously let me have free access to an insight of her unique social circle and provided a first hand, first rate picture of a time gone by. I have been able to include photographs and anecdotes from her own family archives.

Mr Damon Kenneil: My thanks for reuniting me with Vindilis, the boat that started it all and for treating the boat with the respect she deserves.

Mr Bruce Kilpatrick: His loyalty to the Moody product is and always has been appreciated. His time, photos and information he gave me in producing this section of the book has been so helpful.

Premier Marinas Ltd.

Miss Daphne Williamson: My thanks to my Aunt who provided so much background information about the family. This was invaluable in forming a picture of the characters and where they lived.

Mr Gordon Moody: For offering so much support throughout the project. His advice and knowledge was appreciated.

Mr John Moody: For supporting me and adding to the information.

Mr Tony Willey: For supplying a large number of images and for helping me to collate and identify hundreds of other photographs.

Miss Julie Nunn: My PA at Moodys who helped us with our computer literacy.

My children: Beverley, for helping with the editing. James for his computer skills and Jonathan for designing the front and back covers.

Also thanks to the following for their input:

Alan Watson from the Medusa Trust
Philip Simons and Terry Holtham from the World Ships Society Small Craft Group
Mrs Elizabeth Jowett (daughter of Mr Cosby Smallpiece)
Mr Eddie Gillett
Mr Bob Snelgar
Mrs Christine Rolt

Photography:

Beken of Cowes (beken@beken.co.uk)
Imperial War Museum, Photograph Archive
Tom Benn (info@tombenn.com)
Brian Mamby (retired)
Patrick Roach (www.patrick roach.com)
D.B.L. Imaging Bournemouth (info@dbl-imaging.co.uk)
Ajaxnetphoto.com
John Banford Photography (Bishops Waltham)
Norman Burniston Photography (www.burniston.com)
Southern Daily Echo
Front cover: D.B.L. Imaging. Outside back: Tom Benn

Private Photograph Collections

Daphne Williamson
Margaret Williamson
Bruce Kilpatrick
Elizabeth Jowett
Joan Jardine-Brown

References

Lloyds Register of Yachts - 1936 to 1980
Boatbuilding on the River Hamble - A R Moody OBE
St Leonard's church and churchyard, Bursledon

Foreward

Mrs O. Joan Jardine-Brown
Daughter of designer Dr. T. Harrison-Butler

Moody Brothers, later to be known as A.H. Moody & Son Ltd, looked after my father's boats from 1913 until he sold Vindilis in 1939. The boats were Sandook, Clytie, Daydawn, Namoose, Moyzerka and Vindilis. Clytie and Daydawn were houseboats which were owned in succession - Clytie from 1918 until 1919, and Daydawn from 1919 to 1922 or 23. They were used as holiday accommodation for family and friends for whom there was not room aboard Sandook, and were moored just below the toll bridge at Bursledon.

I have no recollection of Clytie, but can remember Daydawn. Namoose, a Lee-on-the Solent one design was owned from 1915 to 1919 and cost £15. She was used for day sailing. When my sister Cynthia and I, the 'afterthought' became old enough to join Sandook's complement, Daydawn was sold. Moyezerka was bought in 1922 as an X-boat and was used for day sailing. After she was sold (1928/29) she was found not to be an authentic X-boat. She gave us some good, if wet, sailing! Sandook was well-used by family and friends, much of it in the Solent. Cruises were made to the West Country and, after a Stuart-Turner was installed in 1932, she went foreign to France, less common then than nowadays.

During all these years Moodys had tended to our boats. My own recollections go back, I suppose to the age of about 3 years - i.e. 1920 and I remember A.H. Moody and his brother Fred and Jack. Jack used to appear now and then in a trap, but whether it was drawn by a donkey or pony, I forget. He had a wooden leg. Then there was Reginald Moody, the 'son' in A.H. Moody & Son. Later still Reginald's sons Alan and Eric. These were the only ones I knew. I also remember Mr Beale in the office who sat on a high stool at a roll top desk and wrote out the bills in longhand.

In September 1934 Sandook was sold and the decision to have Vindilis built was made. My father had waited a long time before he could afford to have a yacht built to one of his own designs, and it coincided with the decision of Moodys to start building yachts in addition to their normal activities which included dinghy building and repairs to larger vessels.

Mr Bunday (although I have hitherto used Christian names, everyone was addressed as 'Mr') was the moving spirit and a very fine craftsman and the standard of building was very high. We used to visit fairly frequently during the months of building until Vindilis was launched on 6th April 1935. That evening there was a supper party in the Parish Rooms at Sarisbury Green for everyone who had been involved with her building, plus members of the Butler family and friends. It was tee total in deference to the Moody's attitude to alcoholic drinks.

Our association with Moodys continued even after the sale of Vindilis in 1939 as both my brothers, Rupert and Eric had boats - Faraway and Seasalter (owned by Rupert and both designed by my father) and Maureen owned by my younger brother Eric.

After a long gap (1938-1975) I had contact with the firm again although infrequently. I feel I have known the firm all my life and although it has changed, it has had to move with the times. Some of the charm has gone, I feel, but charm is not enough in the hard commercial world. I feel very honoured to have been asked to write the foreward to David Moody's excellent archive of his family's firm.

Contents

Part One

Contents

Alexander Herbert Moody

Introduction

Following the successful sale of the business at the end of 2005, it occurred to me that there was very little recorded of the history of A.H. Moody and Son. The Moody family left the premises at midday 21st December 2005 leaving behind a world famous reputation that had been built up over seven generations of continuous management by the family.

I set out to catalogue the boats that had been manufactured at Swanwick. We wanted this as an archive for our immediate family to leave as some kind of legacy. This, of course, was quite a task in itself, but continuing the natural lines of research, things began to snowball and take us along different tangents. Following the loss of a lot of Moody archives in the hurricane of 1987, there was still a way of researching the private yachts built by Moody via the now out of print Lloyds Register of Yachts annual publication, which gave me all the information required. I thought that the wartime archive was lost forever. Not being of an age whereby I was completely computer literate, I sent a number of e-mails and to our excitement people were wishing to help with our research.

I punched the letters HDML (72ft Harbour Defence Motor Launch) into the search engine and up came pages of information. This led to an exchange of e-mails with Alan Watson of the Medusa Trust who said he would be pleased to help, but knew someone who would be better placed to assist, not only with the numbers built, but also when they were completed and what had happened to them whilst in service. I spoke to Philip Simons from the World Ship Society Small Craft Group - who are involved in researching historical craft and locating where they are today. In turn, he communicated with another member, Terry Holtham, and within a few weeks they had all the information that I needed about the wartime craft built by Moodys. It was significant, with some 123 craft from 25ft to 72ft. Filling in this gap made our research more substantial and I began to realise the responsibility of the task in hand.

Having completed the list of craft manufactured at Swanwick, as far as humanly possible, it was suggested that perhaps this document should be published together with the history of the people involved and the development of the Company since 1927. A picture began to emerge of local characters and incidents. I have, where possible, recorded land purchases and events but this is sometimes with a degree of calculated assumption and hear say. No attempt has been made to explain the development and demolition of any buildings on the property due to natural expansion and contraction of the business over the years. In latter years, as manufacturing scaled down, the buildings were adapted so they could be leased to marine-related businesses, therefore creating another form of income. This book deals with the family members involved but by no means does it begin to illustrate the amount of time, hard work and emotion that went into running the business.

There were, of course, good times when things went well, but there were also times of difficulty and regret when hard decisions had to be made. I fondly acknowledge the expertise and loyalty of my family, colleagues and workforce and what they achieved. I hope that readers will find this an accurate and interesting account of the Moody story and believe me, I did my best!

David Moody

I had a charmed childhood in many ways. Born in 1952 to Gordon and Patricia, I grew up with one of the most spectacular views before me from my sitting room window as we lived on Swanwick Shore in Myrtle Cottage. A handful of houseboats provided all the friends I needed, but as I was the only one with a garden, our flowerbeds were always heavily trampled. My father gave up any horticultural aspirations until my brother and I grew up. I was not to realise the significance of the houseboats until later.

Myrtle Cottage, Swanwick Shore, circa. 1950s.

Directly in front of the house were the J-class yachts Endeavour I and II and for a short period, Velsheda, a 19-metre Norada. A little way down river Lulworth was moored. These fantastic yachts had been brought to the river to be laid up by Captain Charlie Bevis who was well known in the racing circles. He lived in a house called "Wisteria" opposite the yard. The house is still there today. In addition to the J-class yachts, there were also a number of ex-Admiralty boats. As a young boy, I thought everyone looked at views like this daily. I didn't realise how lucky I was.

A boatyard full of skilled young men at my disposal also had great advantages for a small boy. I wanted a crossbow? No problem. One was produced but it was so powerful that the arrow could travel from Swanwick Shore over 75 yards to my Grandfather's house in Oslands Lane! Detuning was vital! Model boats, sledges, carnival floats etc. all had the Moody mark. Lucky boy! The disadvantage, of course, was the time my father had to spend at work running the business. Success came at a price.

Another advantage of living on the shore, was the ease to which I could take to the water. Firstly, at six or seven years of age I had a second hand pram dinghy. The public hard was just outside the house. I became an accomplished rower and I would row down the river and then fix up a Jury rig and sail back home. The pram dinghy was soon replaced by an Optimist which Dad built. I remember the International Championships for the Optimist class being hosted by our next door neighbours - Mr and Mrs Smallpiece. It was great. There were no pile moorings in the river so at high tide we had a big expanse of water to play with. As I grew, the Optimist was replaced with an Ian Proctor 'Gull' - I named it 'Twinkle'. I started sailing and raced at Hamble Sailing Club and local regattas at Hamble and Bursledon, picking up a few prizes along the way. For a short while I also went into part ownership of a Merlin Rocket with my brother John.

At the age of 16 I left school and started my apprenticeship as a boat builder. My first week's pay was £4.10.11d! That seemed a lot of money in those days. I began to crew on keel boats and my first experience was aboard a Cutlass 27 with Eric White. This was a prototype with a powdered lead keel so was skittish to say the least. I am surprised it didn't put me off sailing for life. Cutlass II followed with a lead keel and what a fantastic little boat she was. All boats of that size and time appeared to be based on the Folkboat. I then started crewing for Bryan Cozens in a Wayfarer. Bryan was the local harbour master's son and he has only recently retired from racing Wayfarers very successfully. With Bryan, I moved into Jog racing and then into the Soling class.

I loved the Solings. I was in my late teens and I lived for racing at this time. I gave up every weekend and holiday to race aboard a boat called Nimrod, owned by Alec Stone of Salcombe. I crewed with David Hopkins. We competed in many Olympic trials leading up to the fateful Munich Olympic games. We finished in the top six - not being selected to represent the country. Following this, my day job had become so important and demanding that my sailing was put on hold and hasn't come off it yet! From the age of 23, a wife and family of my own took priority.

The famous name was another thing I grew up with and even now, when someone asks my name, I say 'Moody' and the next question often is 'anything to do with boats?' The yard had become an institution and landmark. I chuckle when hearing traffic and travel reports on the radio referring to a jam on the A27 outside Moodys. Don't they know the Company has been sold?

Launching of Pym 1958 typical childhood occasion for me. Spot the 6 year old David with brother John in foreground. Launching staging still very precarious at this time. Photo from David Moody collection.

I have been involved in some wonderful occasions over the years and have met some legendary and fascinating people. Her Royal Highness, the Princess Royal I've been fortunate to have met a few times at various boat shows, but when she came to the Moody Midsummer Meet at Swanwick – we were celebrating the 25-year cooperation with Marine Project Plymouth Ltd – that was the greatest honour. The photograph shows the Princess Royal being introduced to my father in 1997. I remember she flew overhead in a helicopter and landed in the fields adjoining Sarisbury Junior School, much to the delight of the children! She completed her journey to the marina by car and spent a good couple of hours with us, and shared a buffet lunch.

HRH The Princess Royal visits Swanwick Marina for the 1997 Moody Midsummer Meet. Photo from the Southern Daily Echo.

I first met Ellen MacArthur over lunch at the Southampton International Boat Show. I had recently been elected to the Board of National Boat Shows. She was our after dinner speaker and you could not have been anything but captivated by this young lady. Her passion for the sport of sailing was totally infectious. She was without a sponsor at this stage and many of us in the industry pledged our support and help. It was not long after this that Ellen and her management team secured major sponsorship for her planned transatlantic and circumnavigation yacht races. Ellen and I met on numerous occasions following this and she never seemed to forget those people who offered their support to her in those early days. The photograph shows me presenting her with an Honorary President Certificate of the British Marine Federation (South) of which I was Chairman at the time. On the same day she had been to Buckingham Palace to receive her MBE, but she still found time to travel to Cosham to be with us. Ellen had spoken on two occasions at BMF (South) functions and each time drew a capacity audience.

David presenting Ellen with Honorary Presidency of the British Marine Federation (South). Photo by Tony Willey.

Ellen went on to fulfil her ambitions and, for her achievement, was awarded her Damehood which I consider well deserved. She is an inspiration and a true ambassador for the sport.

The River Hamble

The River Hamble originates in the south pond at Bishop's Waltham near the ruins of the Bishop's Palace. There are a number of small springs and streams that flow into this pond. Eventually the pond overflows into a stream which forms the embryonic Hamble River. From here it flows 7.5 miles before entering Southampton Water.

This stream flows from Bishop's Waltham, past Durley and Curdridge, before reaching Botley where it

South pond at Bishop's Waltham with the Bishop's Palace in the background. Photo from David Moody collection.

becomes navigable and tidal. It carries on in a southerly direction and several small tributaries join it on its way. The river passes through the villages of Bursledon, Lower Swanwick, Hamble and Warsash before flowing into Southampton Water. It is crossed at Lower Swanwick by Bridge Road (the A27), the M27 motorway and the Portsmouth to Southampton railway line which was constructed between 1886 and 1888. A second line was added in 1911. Historically, the river was vital for transporting grain, coal and timber and other commodities to Botley and neighbouring villages. It has a long history in boatbuilding and boats were built as far upriver as Botley. It is a river of significance and without doubt the heart of British yachting today.

Before 1800 the only crossings over the river were the ferry between Bursledon and Swanwick and the ford at Botley near the mill. An Act of Parliament in 1797 gave permission for the construction of a wooden bridge and a road between the Itchen river and Park Gate. The bridge and the road were constructed by the Bursledon Bridge Company. The only other crossing was between Hamble and Warsash by a foot ferry that is still operating today - unmissable being painted a shocking pink.

When John Moody settled and started his business he happened to choose a very special part of the river at Swanwick. There is a double bend in the river at this point and the higher banks to the south of this bend gave tremendous weather protection from the south westerly winds which could be very strong from time to time. Years later the company expanded into the area called the Meadows that had once been grazing land.

The stream near Durley. Photo from David Moody collection.

Swanwick Shore where the freshwater spring - The Bunny - enters the Hamble River. The outfall cannot be seen due to the high tide. Photo from Miss D Williamson collection.

The freshwater spring called 'The Bunny', whilst in the Company's ownership, was always a bone of contention. Consideration had to be given to its free flow at all times because of potential flooding which happened regularly. It started off flowing across Moody land as an open ditch, then it was piped, and then at a later date the direction was changed. Planning was always determined by the position of the Bunny.

The uniqueness of this area was also appreciated by other boat and shipbuilders centuries before. Some famous ships like Henry V's flagship the Grace Dieu, was fitted out in the Old Bursledon area and completed in 1418 - one of the largest wooden ships of its time, some 218ft in length. Her remains are still near her birth place, just above the M27 motorway bridge, having been hit by lightning and sadly burnt out.

The photograph below, taken from the south, shows the double bend in the river at Swanwick, the marina and the three bridges. The naturally irrigated marshlands in the bottom right hand corner are where the early ship and boatbuilding took place. It is recorded that three ship and boat builders used the same area, called Bursledon Point. The original was William Wyatt, who built the first HMS Devonshire, launched May 6, 1692. She was blown up on October 10, 1707 following a bloody battle against the French lasting five hours. All crew perished except for two. William Wyatt's life was brought to a premature end when he contracted smallpox and died at the age of 39. The other boat builders who used the same site were Philemon Ewer and later George Parsons. Both are buried in St Leonard's churchyard at Bursledon. Records show Philemon Ewer as building a number of Royal Navy ships - HMS Falkland (48 gun built 1744); HMS Lizard (14gun sloop 1744); HMS Ruby (50gun 1745); HMS Fox (24 gun 1746); HMS Anson (60 gun 1747).

Swanwick Marina, photographed from the south showing the special double bend in the river that made this site so unique. The river meanders northward under the three bridges. Photo from D.B.L. Imaging

George Parsons was responsible for the build of HMS Fox (1780); HMS Quebec (32 gun 1781); HMS Ardent (64 gun 1782); HMS Phoenix (36 gun 1783); HMS Elephant (74 gun 1786); HMS Dover (44 gun 1786); HMS Diligence (1795); HMS Galatea (1797); HMS Cambrian (1797); HMS Penelope (36 gun 1798); HMS Jason(1800); HMS Resistance (1801); HMS Apollo (38 gun 1803); HMS Tribune (1803); HMS Fly (1804); HMS Horatio (1807). There is a painting that illustrates clearly the building of large ships off Lands End in the sedge land in the corner of the river. It is by the artist J. Forbes (1810). It is said that the masts were stored and dressed in the Mews alongside Victory cottages at Swanwick Shore.

The river partially frozen over 1895. The picture is in the region of the Jolly Sailor. Old Bursledon. Photo from Miss D Williamson collection.

Having lived and worked on the Hamble all my life, I have seen it in many different moods. Tides can be very variable - especially spring tides which have caused the majority of the site to be flooded on the top of the tide from time to time depending on factors such as wind direction, barometric pressure and strength etc.. We have had mild winters of late, but everyone remembers the severe winter of 1963. Snow arrived on Boxing Day and was still with us in March. The river actually froze, apart from the central stream and the ice was so thick that it supported the weight of a man. I can even recall floating downstream on a piece of ice that had broken away. This was quickly followed by

my childhood friend, Eric Gillett, in a dinghy who was looking after my well being! When I look back, I certainly took some risks. I'm glad my parents were blissfully unaware! The photograph is taken from Shore Road in the area of the old slipways looking out towards the creek where The Bunny used to flow.

It is also recorded that there was another cold spell that caused the river to partially freeze over and that was in 1895.

Two people can be seen walking on the ice which is thick enough to support their weight, 1963. Photo from David Moody collection.

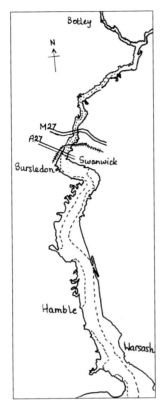

The rough diagram shows the course of the Hamble River from Botley and illustrates the recent M27 motorway bridge, the railway bridge which was constructed in 1888 and also the A27 concrete bridge which was built in the early 30s and adopted by the local authority. Prior to this there was a wooden toll bridge belonging to the Bursledon Bridge Company. Before this there was a ferry which was sometimes precarious that crossed between Bursledon and Swanwick. This proved a valuable artery for commerce as transport improved. The diagram shows the double bend in the river between Bursledon and Swanwick and the sedge lands opposite Swanwick that were used in the construction of many naval vessels over the centuries.

Diagram showing the Hamble River from Botley in the north to its entrance at Southampton water.

The original wooden Bursledon Bridge and tollgate with the Red Lion public house in white on the left-hand side, circa. 1900 Photo from Miss D Williamson collection.

Swanwick Shore in the area of the original boatyard, circa. 1900. Photo from Miss D Williamson collection.

The Moody Family

John Moody was the start of it all. He was orphaned and moved to Swanwick Lane from the Moorgreen area of South Stoneham near Southampton, around the year 1827. In 1832 he married his wife Elizabeth, and set up home near the entrance to the lane on Bridge Road. Little is known of John's ancestry. The Census of 1851 notes the family. His trade was recorded as a fisherman and four children are mentioned - Alexander, Louisa, Cliff and Henry. His brother-in-law, John Goddard, also lodged with them.

There is a triangle of land to the west entrance of Swanwick Shore Road and he began his trade of repair and maintenance of boats on a strip of that land alongside the Bursledon Bridge Company. He also began to build small dinghies on the site. Some 30 years later he purchased this strip of land measuring 93ft by 24ft officially shown in the plan (on page 25) and legend has it he paid £25. His eldest son, Alexander, joined him and continued to build the business with his father but there is no record of any other family member involvement. John died in 1880 at the age of 67.

Alexander Moody with his penny farthing bicycle, circa. 1870. Photo from Miss D Williamson collection.

Alexander, born in 1838, married Ellen Freemantle and had four sons, Alexander Herbert (always known as Herbert), Frederick, Walter and Jack. Three daughters are also mentioned. They lived in Clematis Cottage which was adjacent to the yard, facing Bridge Road next to a chapel in Key Lane. The chapel remains, but the cottage was demolished as the business expanded. He later moved to a larger house, Avalon, to the west of the entrance to Swanwick Lane. Alexander loved sailing and had his own fishing type gaff cutter, 'Onward'. She had a square stern and a transom hung rudder. His failing sight in later years meant that his grandson, Reginald was needed to escort him. Alexander died in 1919.

Herbert and Frederick both joined Alexander in the boatbuilding business, Herbert having previously qualified as a blacksmith in Sylvesters at Park Gate. After Alexander's death, Fred and Herbert continued the business as a partnership, known as A.H. and F. Moody. Walter and Jack, together with the daughters, did not join the business although Jack helped out as a joiner from time to time.

Alexander Herbert Moody married Elizabeth Harriet Burt and settled in Myrtle Cottage in Swanwick Shore Road. Herbert borrowed £200 to build the house in 1884. This house was later sold to grandson, Gordon who owns it to this day! Herbert and Elizabeth had two children, Effie and Reginald.

Frederick lived in a bungalow opposite Oslands Farm (now The Ship Inn) in Lower Swanwick with his wife, Ada and daughter Eva. He was a shipwright, according to the Census. On his retirement, he moved to the Sarisbury Green area.

Effie Moody with mother, Elizabeth outside Myrtle Cottage circa. 1910. Photo from Miss D Williamson collection.

Reginald joined the company when he was 16, learning the trade and qualifying as a shipwright.

Reginald married a local girl, Charlotte Elsie in 1912 and they raised a family of six children - three boys and three girls. All three sons eventually joined the business. Reginald worked alongside his father and uncle until the outbreak of the First World War. Reginald failed his medical, so worked for the war effort at Camper and Nicholsons both at Gosport and Southampton. Herbert and Frederick were meanwhile continuing to work at Swanwick with a skeleton staff maintaining a great number of private yachts

A.H. Moody with coil of rope, hauling boat from water, circa. 1900. Photo from Miss D Williamson collection.

laid up during this period. They were also instructed to remove various metals from the boats for the war effort. These were turbulent times, but the Company was able to survive.

The partnership of A.H. and F. Moody continued and the main activities included the laying up and repair of boats, building small dinghies and work on larger sailing vessels in neighbouring ports. The vessels from the many local industries also needed maintenance and the company serviced and repaired coal barges, grain vessels, fishing vessels and timber barges as well as carrying out work on Stella, Cupid and Gem, part of the crabbing fleet at Warsash. These craft had wooden compartments which were constructed by us. The compartments filled with water for the well being of the crabs and lobsters whilst in transit. Every so often the fleet required underwater maintenance and this was done at Woolston. Another activity that the company was involved in was the maintenance and repair of the then wooden river toll bridge which remained in private hands until it was adopted by Hampshire County Council and rebuilt in concrete and completed in 1934.

The photograph shows the wooden Bursledon Bridge and the toll house together with the five chimneys of the old Bursledon Brickworks in the background. These were affectionately known as the 'five sisters'. As a point of interest, Mr George Parsons, a local Bursledon shipbuilder, was an original investor in the Bursledon Bridge Company around 1800 and it is recorded that the first year's tolls totalled £126. In 1815, the Battle of Waterloo resulted in an increase of military traffic, takings rose to over £2,000. George Parsons is buried in St Leonard's Church at Bursledon and a plaque states that he was a shipbuilder of some renown. Many ships were built but among them was a 74-gun warship named HMS Elephant which was Lord Nelson's flagship at the battle of Copenhagen. Building took place on the other side of the river from Moodys, on the marshes just off Lands End at Bursledon.

Original wooden Bursledon Bridge. Note tollhouse and the 'Five sisters' chimneys of the Bursledon Brickworks in the background. Photo from Joan Jardine-Brown collection.

In 1932 the Moody partnership was dissolved on Frederick's retirement and the brothers went their separate ways. From this time, the company on Swanwick Shore became known as A.H. Moody and Son. Shortly after the formation of the new company, Herbert and Reginald were joined by a young Alan. He trained as a marine engineer within the business, under the direction of Mr Harold Daish.

New yacht Nyala being pulled out of the original building shed on Swanwick Shore, circa. 1936.
Photo from David Moody collection.

After completing his training, Alan joined the office staff and the business continued to expand into yacht chandlery, repairs, maintenance and consideration was seriously given to the manufacture of larger private yachts. There was apprehension about this from some quarters of the family, but eventually this was overcome. The mandate was given that any yacht built would be of the highest quality and consequently the first yacht to be built was completed in 1935 and was named Vindilis, to a design of Dr T. Harrison-Butler. Eighteen quality yachts were built at this time, prior to the outbreak of the Second World War.

The Company became 'Incorporated' on 27th August 1935. The inaugural Board of Directors consisted of Alexander Herbert (Chairman), Reginald Herbert (Director), Mrs Effie Williamson (Non executive Director) and Alan (Director). Herbert, the Chairman, retained his directorship until his death in 1951. Reginald retained his directorship until his death on 26 December 1974. Alan also served as Chairman and Managing Director for many years, retiring in 1981.

The decision to go into manufacturing was partly due to Mr Eddy Bunday - a highly experienced craftsman and manager. The manufacturing of these early boats was carried out in a shed that had been erected on the original site, sector 1 (see page 25). Later, after leasing some land on sector 6, some larger open-sided sheds were built to accommodate the manufacture of bigger yachts. When war broke out, the larger Admiralty boats were all built on this sector. It was also at this point that sector 5 was requisitioned by the Admiralty as a repair facility for landing craft and many other Admiralty vessels. It then became connected to HMS Cricket.

The Admiralty built a large slipway which proved to be very useful on the return of the property following the War.

Large group photograph circa. 1938 in front of offices and original building shed. Young Gordon Moody cross legged on floor in front aged 12. Behind him is A.H. Moody, to his right is Reginald, Eric and Roy Williamson, to his left Mr Bunday and Alan.
Photo from Miss D Williamson collection.

11

Reginald's sister, Effie also played a part in the company. She had married and had a son, Roy and daughter, Daphne. Effie retired as a Director in 1977. Roy joined the company and qualified as a marine engineer, again under the direction of Harold Daish. He stayed at Swanwick until he served with the RAF throughout the War. On his discharge, he rejoined the company as a Director until his retirement in 1981.

Launching of Lady Christabel with building sheds in background 1938. Photo from Miss D Williamson collection.

Naturally the outbreak of war had a profound effect on the entire area. All private yachts in build had to be put on hold. These were laid up for the duration together with all other yachts. As a skilled reserved occupation, Moodys were in extremely great demand and were immediately fully involved in the war effort. The labour force increased dramatically totalling probably an estimated 200 people. There were boat builders, joiners, marine engineers, electricians, painters and labourers. Many of these were local women determined to play their part. It was hard, necessary work of very long hours.

Records show that during this time Moodys built dozens of Admiralty craft. This included Harbour Defence Motor Launches (HDMLs); MSBs; MFBs; MPPs; HLs; MCs; MSTs; MFVs and LCAs. The company took great pride in acknowledging that their craft were operating in the major events of the War. The boatyard miraculously evaded any bomb damage even though an obvious target - unlike similar yards like Camper and Nicholsons at Gosport.

Another major activity for the Company during the War was the refit and repairs of damaged Admiralty craft of all descriptions. These repairs literally totalled thousands. It is also recorded that many private motor yachts were acquisitioned by the Admiralty. One in particular, Lady Christabel, was built for Sir Morris Jenks and was requisitioned. She attended and safely returned from Dunkirk in 1940.

In March 1943, Eric Herbert joined the Board of Directors at the age of 21, following his training as a boat builder. He went on to become Chairman of the company in 1981 following Alan's retirement. He remained as Chairman until his untimely death in 1985.

Four generations. Seated in wheelchair, A.H. Moody.
Behind, left to right, Eric holding eldest son, Michael, father Reginald, Alan and Gordon, circa. 1945. Photo from David Moody collection.

Gordon Moody, the youngest of Reginald's sons also joined the workforce during the War. In 1939 he began his apprenticeship as a boat builder at the tender age of 14 and later went on to work as a joiner. Gordon enjoyed the skilled practical work and he was responsible for converting a number of HDMLs into private yachts following the War. There were three recorded in the Lloyds Register of Yachts - Lady Walrus (ex HDML 1278) owner Sir Edward T. Peel KBE DSO MC; Moreta owner H. A. White and Viloanda owner Mr H. E. Bradley. There were other conversions on Admiralty craft following their disposal following the War.

Gordon obtained his Directorship in April 1946 and became Managing Director in 1981 and then Chairman in 1985, following his brother Eric's death. Gordon had a passion for the hands-on work of construction and always worked closely with the workforce. He played an important part in the development of the property, often working in overalls early in the day with the men, overseeing the building of slipways, sheds and boats. He would still be seen doing this well after his retirement!

In future years, the three brothers - Alan, Eric, Gordon and their cousin Roy found four natural paths within the company, which worked extremely well. Alan was the figurehead, dealing with matters concerning expansion of the industry and training. He represented the industry widely and was rewarded with the OBE for his services. Eric became adept in obtaining contracts for new boats and repair yard contracts whilst developing new procedures for launching and lifting boats. Also acquired at this time was a boat that was converted into a refuelling vessel, an ex NAAFI supply boat that had been on service in Scapa Flow. She was called 'Bosun!' She travelled up and down the river and as far a field as the Isle of Wight, refuelling the ever increasing boating population. She also carried items of food and chandlery. This service continued until shore side facilities were set up.

Old joiner shop in Swanwick Shore. Gordon Moody and Arthur Boyce working at benches in the 1950's. Photo from Gordon Moody collection.

Gordon still remained very hands-on. He found his niche in new construction, boat sales and the ongoing development of the property. Roy worked in the administration of the company.

It was during the years following the War that the Company obtained much more land on Swanwick Shore, stretching from the Shore to Bursledon Bridge. With the amount of finance available to them, one has to acknowledge the extraordinary foresight they had as the land developed from patches of land between marshland to a full 23 acres of reclaimed leasehold and freehold property. This acquisition of land was to accommodate the expansion of the marine business in all areas. This included yacht manufacture, GRP

and wood; repair yard facilities (including launching, lifting, storing and repairing of boats;) the development of a 350-berth marina; chandlery and new and used boat sales. We laid and maintained many deep water swinging moorings as well as mud berths. These moorings became a very important part of the business. All this brought the company forward to one of the most innovative and famous companies in the industry.

Family members working in the company, circa. 1973
Left to Right: Tony, Christopher, David, John, Gordon, Eric, Alan, Roy Williamson and Graham. Pictured on the old jetty, Swanwick Shore. Photo from David Moody collection.

The next generation continued to expand the business and again found their own natural paths. Alan's son, Graham was appointed to the Board in July 1974, having spent time with Frederick Parker's design office and learning practical boatbuilding skills. He became responsible for new construction and later service and repairs.

John, Gordon's eldest son, took another direction. He trained in boat sales under Arthur Pitfield who had joined the company as a joiner prior to the Second World War. After the war, Arthur became the company yacht broker. John then went to America and spent time with the Richard Bertram Corporation in Florida. On his return he was always looking for new sales opportunities. John was appointed to the Board in 1977. He was Director and Chairman on Gordon's retirement.

I joined the company from school. Again, practical like my father, I completed my apprenticeship in boatbuilding and worked on the last Moody built wooden boat - Swan Dancer. I moved into brokerage and continued in this, expanding the department and introducing Used Boat Shows to the industry. I stayed in sales, and was appointed to the Board in July 1982. I was involved in all areas of sales - including motorboats Fairline, Princess, and latterly the Moody production range.

Whilst families undoubtedly have 'their moments', when it mattered the branches of this family all pulled together and supported each other in their quest to improve and expand the business, until its eventual sale in 2005.

Several other members of the next generation started their careers in the business and showed great promise. They were all appointed to the Board at an early age. Graham's sons - Martin and Scott were working alongside their father in boat yard management and a further branch of manufacturing pre-fabricated teak decks for production yachts. Graham's nephew, Sean Noble had been working with me in continuing to build a successful used boat sales department. My son, James had joined the company from college and also worked in sales. All four of this generation are still employed in the marine industry.

Eddy Bunday and Reginald Moody, circa. 1960 in front of the manager's office, Swanwick Shore.
Photo from David Moody collection.

I should also acknowledge that Eric's sons, Christopher and Tony worked in the Company for a time. Christopher worked alongside his father in the repair yard in the 1980s until his father's death, when Christopher took the helm. In the early 90s Christopher decided to leave the company to follow career aspirations. His brother, Tony, went into the chandlery side of the company and expanded it considerably. He also chose to leave and relocated to Spain in the early 90s.

Whilst primarily a family concern, many people contributed to the successful running of the firm throughout its existence. Other directors, managers and foremen included:

- *Dennis Sessions* – executive director, who was involved in developing the marina
- *David Stewart* – executive director in charge of finances for many years
- *Peter Allsebrook* – who was non-executive director
- *Philip Wright* – also non-executive director
- *Christine Rolt* – non executive director and Effie Williamson's granddaughter
- *Bob Jubb* – executive director and company accountant
- *Richard Lewis* – company secretary
- *Trevor Allen* – company secretary
- *Eddy Bunday* – yard manager in all but name in the early 1920s responsible for the development of building wooden boats. He retired in 1965.

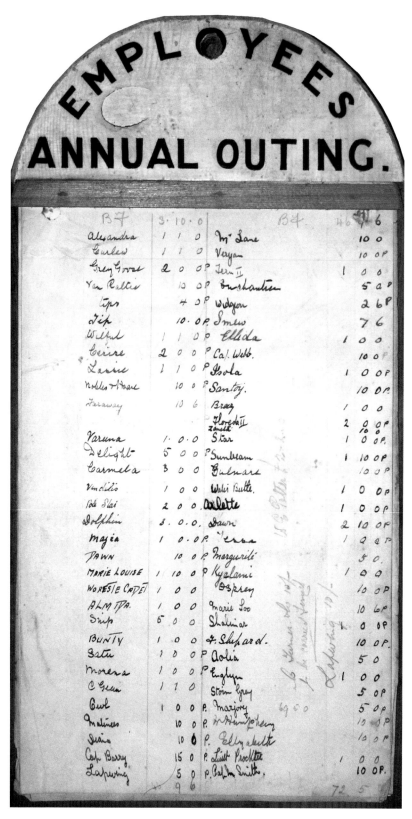

Notice Board recording donations towards the annual outing of the workforce, circa. 1935.

This notice board was kindly passed on to me by the new owners of the yard. It used to be displayed in the building shed. It gives five years of records showing donations towards the annual employees works outing. These are from owners and customers. The sheet showing is of 1935 and you will note generous donations from the owners of Delight and Vindilis. It must have been some outing for £72 in 1935!

Those who have worked for the company and lived in the vicinity would have been well aware of the siren that used to mark the start of the working day, tea breaks, lunch and end of day. If this wasn't enough, there would be another siren at 7.28am and 12.48pm to warn of the pending siren of the start of work!! As I lived so close to the yard, I didn't move from bed until the first siren. I had little excuse for being late!

At the start of the company it is recorded that everyone lived so close to the yard that no one would have had more than a five-minute walk to their place of employment. It is interesting that this trend continued until the sale of the company. Eric lived at Warsash for a while and his four miles was the furthest commute in the history of Moodys. It is also interesting to note that all members of the family, without exception, drove to work!

Photo from Miss D Williamson collection.

Photo from Miss D Williamson collection.

Group photograph, above, taken in the area of the earliest land purchase by John Moody on Swanwick Shore. Photo shows young Alan Moody seated on Reginald's right, circa 1923. Alan must have been a frequent visitor to the boatyard after school as he seems to be totally at ease amongst the men. Alan is obviously 'one of the boys!' Although I cannot personally identify these men, they should be named on the wages ledger of the 1920s, mentioned earlier and illustrated on pages 19 and 20. How times have changed. Tobacco certainly was socially acceptable then! The flat caps were also a vital fashion statement!

The photo left, is of Reginald Moody with his father, Alexander Herbert pictured in front of the single-storey building on Swanwick Shore at the entrance to the creek. This building was demolished fairly early on in the company's development.

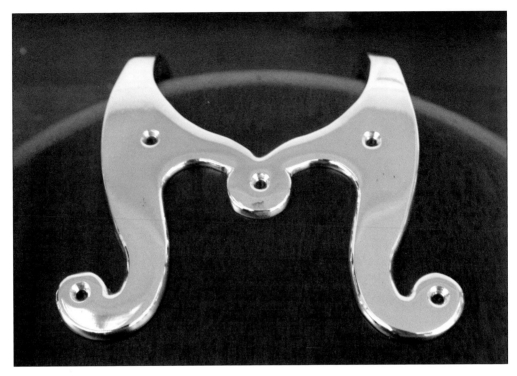

Where have I seen this before? Photo from SeaSure Ltd.

You may think 'where have I seen this before?' It was, of course, the hinge of the toilet cover of the famous Baby Blake toilet made at the Sunbeam works in Gosport, by Blakes. This toilet was widely used in our early wooden yachts. My Grandfather, Reginald, assisted in the tooling of this hinge which was designed in the shape of the letter 'M' for Moody. Whether he had freedom of choice over this or if this was done by design, I will never know. The toilet is still being manufactured, although not by Blakes, and the letter 'M' remains to this day.

Following are copies of random pages taken from the original wages ledger dating from 1913 through to 1920 (the period spanning the First World War). You will see the change in numbers of employees from the outbreak of war to the resumption of peacetime in 1918. You will note that I have mentioned Jack Moody, Herbert's brother, earlier as having worked for the Company from time to time. It would appear that this would have been for the duration of the First World War and that Reginald Moody had worked for Camper and Nicholsons. This must have been on a subcontract basis as he was still on the payroll of A.H. & F. Moody. Payday was obviously Saturday.

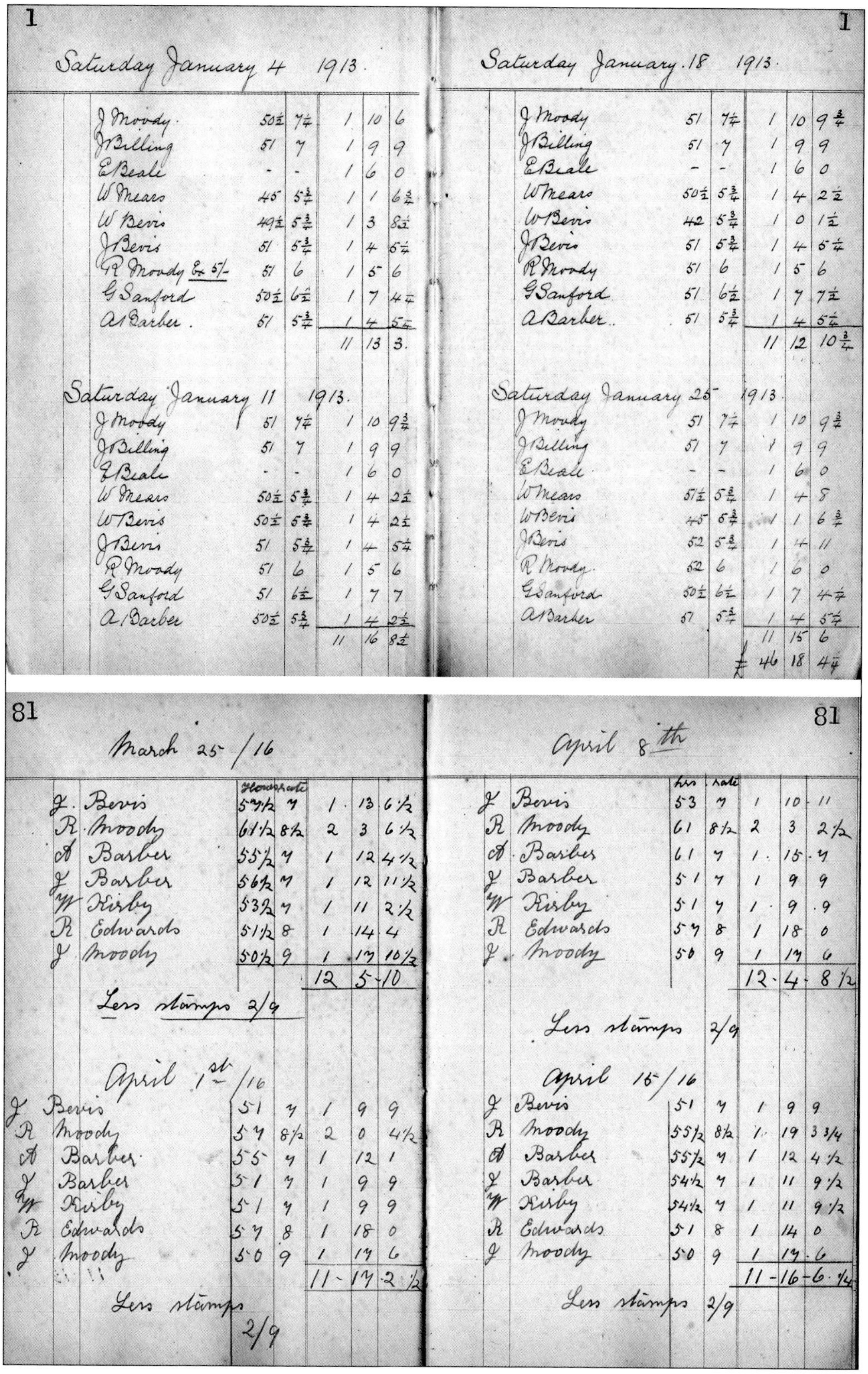

1

Saturday January 4 1913.

J Moody	50½	7¼	1	10	6
J Billing	51	7	1	9	9
E Beale	-	-	1	6	0
W Mears	45	5¾	1	1	6¾
W Bevis	49½	5¾	1	3	8½
J Bevis	51	5¾	1	4	5¼
R Moody Ex 5/-	51	6	1	5	6
G Sanford	50½	6½	1	7	4¼
A Barber.	51	5¾	1	4	5¼
			11	13	3.

Saturday January 11 1913.

J Moody	51	7¼	1	10	9¾
J Billing	51	7	1	9	9
E Beale	-	-	1	6	0
W Mears	50½	5¾	1	4	2½
W Bevis	50½	5¾	1	4	2½
J Bevis	51	5¾	1	4	5¼
R Moody	51	6	1	5	6
G Sanford	51	6½	1	7	7
A Barber	50½	5¾	1	4	2½
			11	16	8½

1

Saturday January. 18 1913.

J Moody	51	7¼	1	10	9¾
J Billing	51	7	1	9	9
E Beale	-	-	1	6	0
W Mears	50½	5¾	1	4	2½
W Bevis	42	5¾	1	0	1½
J Bevis	51	5¾	1	4	5¼
R Moody	51	6	1	5	6
G Sanford	51	6½	1	7	7½
A Barber..	51	5¾	1	4	5¼
			11	12	10¾

Saturday January 25 1913.

J Moody	51	7¼	1	10	9¾
J Billing	51	7	1	9	9
E Beale	-	-	1	6	0
W Mears	51½	5¾	1	4	8
W Bevis	45	5¾	1	1	6¾
J Bevis	52	5¾	1	4	11
R Moody	52	6	1	6	0
G Sanford	50½	6½	1	7	4¼
A Barber	51	5¾	1	4	5¼
			11	15	6
			£ 46	18	4¼

81

March 25 /16

	Hours	Rate			
J. Bevis	57½	7	1.	13	6½
R. Moody	61½	8½	2	3	6½
A Barber	55½	7	1	12	4½
J Barber	56½	7	1	12	11½
W Kirby	53½	7	1	11	2½
R Edwards	51½	8	1	14	4
J Moody	50½	9	1	17	10½
			12	5-	10

Less stamps 2/9

April 1st /16

J Bevis	51	7	1	9	9
R Moody	57	8½	2	0	4½
A Barber	55	7	1	12	1
J Barber	51	7	1	9	9
W Kirby	51	7	1	9	9
R Edwards	57	8	1	18	0
J Moody	50	9	1	17	6
			11-	17	2 ½

Less stamps 2/9

81

April 8th

	Hrs	Rate			
J Bevis	53	7	1	10-	11
R Moody	61	8½	2	3	2½
A Barber	61	7	1.	15-	7
J Barber	51	7	1	9	9
W Kirby	51	7	1.	9	9
R Edwards	57	8	1	18	0
J Moody	50	9	1	17	6
			12-	4-	8½

Less stamps 2/9

April 15/16

J Bevis	51	7	1	9	9
R Moody	55½	8½	1	19	3¾
A Barber	55½	7	1	12	4½
J Barber	54½	7	1	11	9½
W Kirby	54½	7	1	11	9½
R Edwards	51	8	1	14	0
J Moody	50	9	1	17	6
			11-	16-	6. ¼

Less stamps 2/9

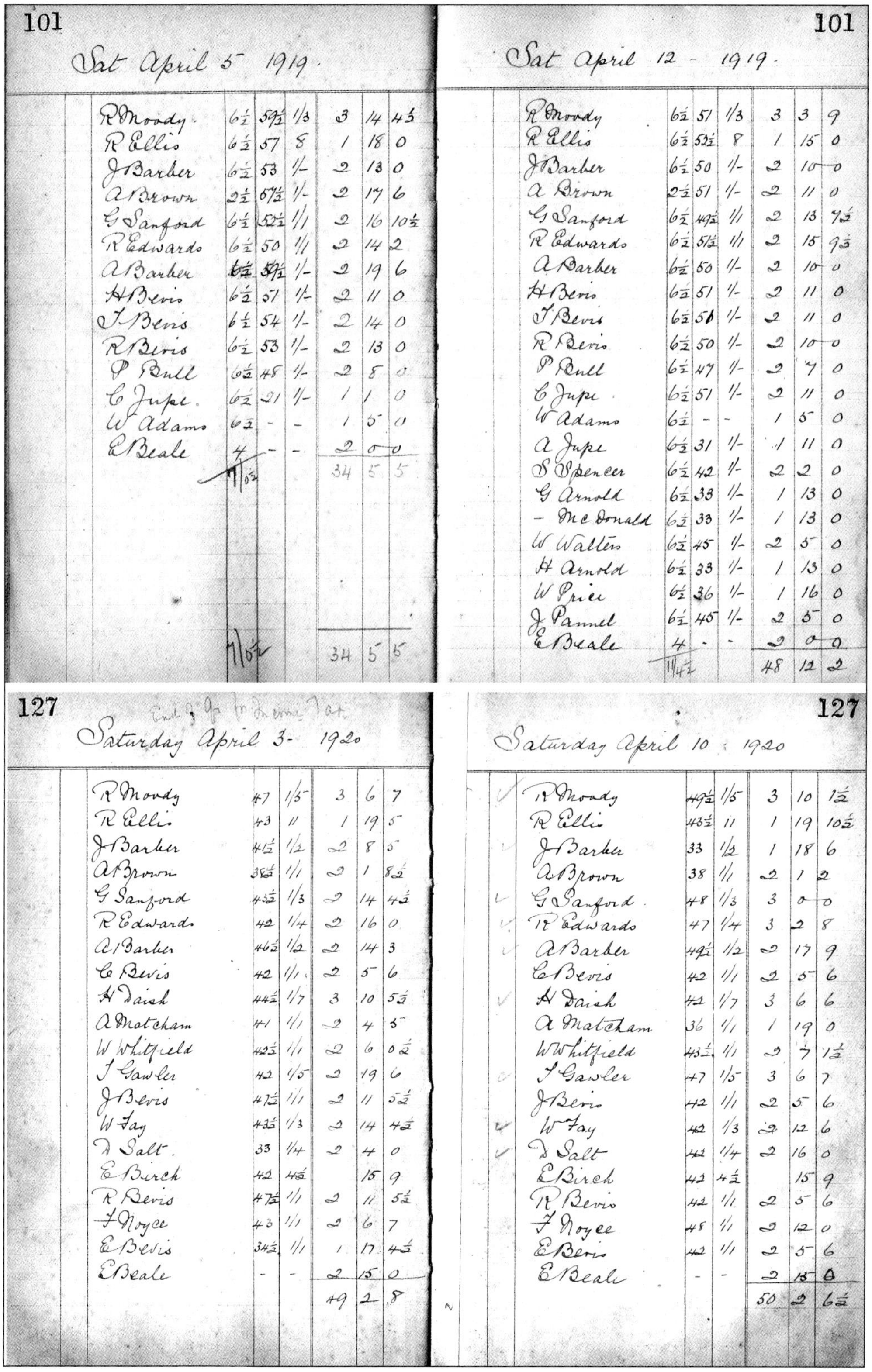

The Moody Legacy 1827-2005

101 — Sat April 5 1919

Name				£	s	d
R Moody	6½	59½	1/3	3	14	4½
R Ellis	6½	57	8	1	18	0
J Barber	6½	53	1/-	2	13	0
A Brown	2½	67½	1/-	2	17	6
G Sanford	6½	52½	1/1	2	16	10½
R Edwards	6½	50	1/1	2	14	2
A Barber	6½	59½	1/-	2	19	6
H Bevis	6½	51	1/-	2	11	0
J Bevis	6½	54	1/-	2	14	0
R Bevis	6½	53	1/-	2	13	0
P Bull	6½	48	1/-	2	8	0
C Jupe	6½	21	1/-	1	1	0
W Adams	6½	-	-	1	5	0
E Beale	4	-	-	2	0	0
				34	5	5

101 — Sat April 12 1919

Name				£	s	d
R Moody	6½	51	1/3	3	3	9
R Ellis	6½	52½	8	1	15	0
J Barber	6½	50	1/-	2	10	0
A Brown	2½	51	1/-	2	11	0
G Sanford	6½	49½	1/1	2	13	7½
R Edwards	6½	51½	1/1	2	15	9½
A Barber	6½	50	1/-	2	10	0
H Bevis	6½	51	1/-	2	11	0
J Bevis	6½	51	1/-	2	11	0
R Bevis	6½	50	1/-	2	10	0
P Bull	6½	47	1/-	2	7	0
C Jupe	6½	51	1/-	2	11	0
W Adams	6½	-	-	1	5	0
A Jupe	6½	31	1/-	1	11	0
S Spencer	6½	42	1/-	2	2	0
G Arnold	6½	33	1/-	1	13	0
- McDonald	6½	33	1/-	1	13	0
W Walters	6½	45	1/-	2	5	0
H Arnold	6½	33	1/-	1	13	0
W Price	6½	36	1/-	1	16	0
J Pannel	6½	45	1/-	2	5	0
E Beale	4	-	-	2	0	0
				48	12	2

127 — Saturday April 3 1920

Name			£	s	d
R Moody	47	1/5	3	6	7
R Ellis	43	11	1	19	5
J Barber	41½	1/2	2	8	5
A Brown	38½	1/1	2	1	8½
G Sanford	44½	1/3	2	14	4½
R Edwards	42	1/4	2	16	0
A Barber	46½	1/2	2	14	3
C Bevis	42	1/1	2	5	6
H Daish	44½	1/7	3	10	5½
A Matcham	41	1/1	2	4	5
W Whitfield	40½	1/1	2	6	0½
J Gawler	42	1/5	2	19	6
J Bevis	47½	1/1	2	11	5½
W Fay	43½	1/3	2	14	4½
D Salt	33	1/4	2	4	0
E Birch	42	4½		15	9
R Bevis	47½	1/1	2	11	5½
J Noyce	43	1/1	2	6	7
E Bevis	34½	1/1	1	17	4½
E Beale	-	-	2	15	0
			49	2	8

127 — Saturday April 10 1920

Name			£	s	d
R Moody	49½	1/5	3	10	1½
R Ellis	43½	11	1	19	10½
J Barber	33	1/2	1	18	6
A Brown	38	1/1	2	1	2
G Sanford	48	1/3	3	0	0
R Edwards	47	1/4	3	2	8
A Barber	49½	1/2	2	17	9
C Bevis	42	1/1	2	5	6
H Daish	42	1/7	3	6	6
A Matcham	36	1/1	1	19	0
W Whitfield	43½	1/1	2	7	1½
J Gawler	47	1/5	3	6	7
J Bevis	42	1/1	2	5	6
W Fay	42	1/3	2	12	6
D Salt	42	1/4	2	16	0
E Birch	42	4½		15	9
R Bevis	42	1/1	2	5	6
J Noyce	48	1/1	2	12	0
E Bevis	42	1/1	2	5	6
E Beale	-	-	2	15	0
			50	2	6½

20

A. H. Moody and Son.

30. September 1931.

A. J. Palmer, F.S.A.A.

Incorporated Accountant.

Fareham, Hants.

A. H and F. Moody.

Dissolution A/cs. 16 January 1932.

A. J. Palmer, F.S.A.A.
Incorporated Accountant.
Fareham, Hants.

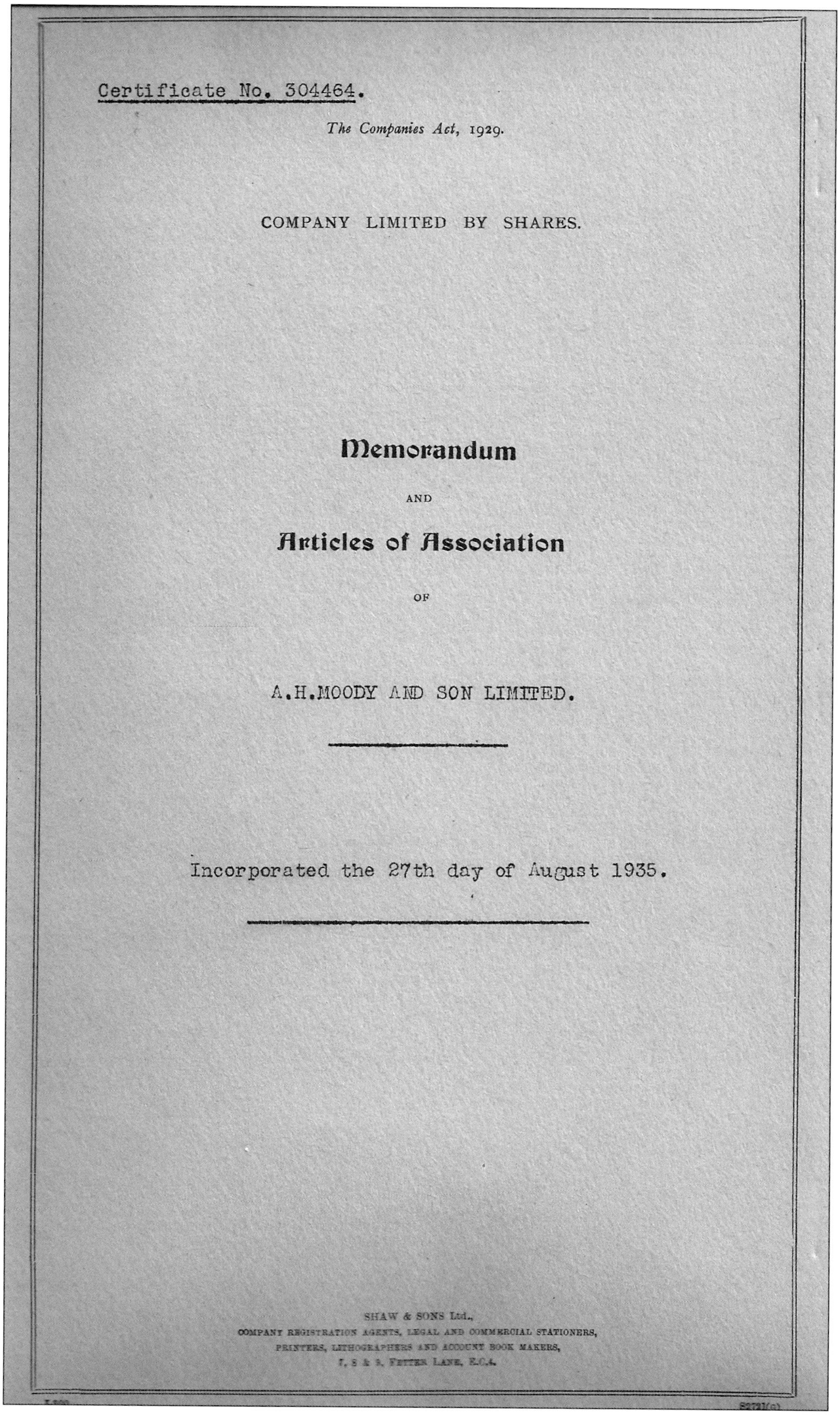

Certificate No. 304464.

The Companies Act, 1929.

COMPANY LIMITED BY SHARES.

Memorandum

AND

Articles of Association

OF

A.H.MOODY AND SON LIMITED.

———————————

Incorporated the 27th day of August 1935.

———————————

SHAW & SONS Ltd.,
COMPANY REGISTRATION AGENTS, LEGAL AND COMMERCIAL STATIONERS,
PRINTERS, LITHOGRAPHERS AND ACCOUNT BOOK MAKERS,
7, 8 & 9, FETTER LANE, E.C.4.

No. 304464.

Copy.

CERTIFICATE OF INCORPORATION.

———————————————

I HEREBY CERTIFY That A.H.MOODY AND SON LIMITED

is this day Incorporated under the Companies Act,

1929, and that the Company is LIMITED.

GIVEN under my hand at London this Twenty-seventh

day of August One thousand nine hundred and thirty-five.

F.GREENWOOD,

Registrar of Companies.

The Acquisition & Disposal of Land

The plan is an attempt to explain the expansion of Moody's boatyard. Scales and proportions may not be accurate. We have already mentioned that John Moody acquired *sector 1* (93' x 24') on his arrival to the area and this was eventually to be the site of the first building shop. This was shortly followed by *sector 2* which was purchased from the Bursledon Bridge Company. *Sector 3* was acquired by purchasing various small parcels of land from private individuals. This area was mainly residential. Three houses and gardens were purchased from the Mears family and then Clematis Cottage (B), which was owned by the Gillett family. All these houses were demolished to make way for the housing of ancillary skills such as plumbing, electrical etc. The nearby chapel (C) remains to this day.

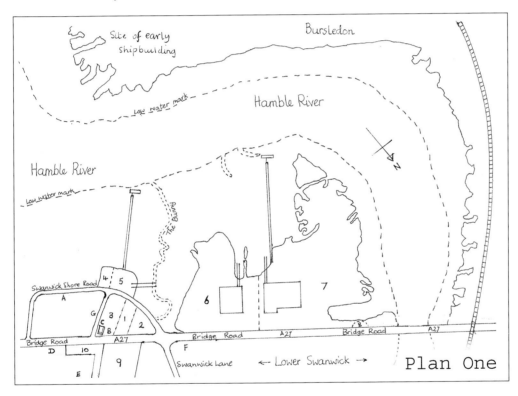

A - Myrtle Cottage

B - Clematis Cottage

C - Chapel

D - Frederick Moody's House

E - Reg Moody's house

F - Alexander Moody's House

G - Victory Cottages

Plan of area around boatyard showing features of note.

1. *Original site purchased by John Moody*
2. *Land purchased from Bursledon Bridge Company*
3. *Land purchased from private individuals*
4. *Land purchased from Swanwick Coal Company*
5. *Land purchased from the Board of Trade*
6. *Land purchased from Cooper's Brewery*
7. *Land purchased in stages in 1962 & 1966*
8. *Old Tollhouse purchased from private individual*
9. *Land known as the Abbey*
10. *Land purchased from Reg Moody for petrol station.*

The Gillett family also owned a house in sector one which later became the offices. Research shows that Emma, Alexander Moody's youngest daughter and Herbert's sister married Ambrose Ralph Gillett. This union brought these two families together. A grandson of Ambrose, Eddie Gillett, now in his mid-nineties, still lives in Victory Cottages on his own having been widowed many years ago. It is quite extraordinary that the villages consisted of a handful of families who became inter-related and it would appear that the main families of Swanwick were the Bevises, Moodys and Gilletts. It is still the case today.

Sector 4 was purchased from the Swanwick Coal Company which, incidentally, was operated by the Mears family. *Sector 5* was purchased from the Board of Trade. This housed stabling for the Coal Company and later Moody's chandlery which was on the first floor. As mentioned, sector 5 was requisitioned at the start of Second World War and became part of HMS Cricket which maintained landing craft and other Admiralty vessels. Following the War it was returned and later accommodated the main building shed and slipway. *Sector 6* was originally leased and then purchased from Cooper's Brewery in 1936. In 1937, Moodys built a large building shop with open sides. This was used for the manufacturing of bigger craft and, during the War, the larger Admiralty boats. These open sides were eventually filled in to make it more secure.

Sector 7 was purchased in two stages. The first was acquired in 1962 and the remainder in 1966. *Sectors 6* and *7* were always known by the family and workforce as 'The Meadow' as in times past these had been grazing fields for horses and cattle. As a point of interest, this land was also used for the Bursledon Regatta Fair that took place every year.

Sector 8 was finally purchased from a private individual as this went into private ownership following the sale of the Toll House. In 1955, it was decided to purchase a plot of land from Reginald Moody to accommodate a petrol station and some lock up garages. The planning permission, however, was not secured easily but following the success of this venture, it was sold in 1969 to the Regent Oil Company. This is shown as *Sector 10*.

Sector 9 was purchased earlier and accommodated some low lying buildings that were acquired from Fareham and reassembled on the site. This was always affectionately known as 'The Abbey' as the building structure resembled a church building. This sector was sold in 1972.

Finally the company purchased another boatyard at Warsash from Woodnutt and Co Ltd. in December 1963. This had previously been known as the Tormentor Yacht Station and latterly 'Stone Pier'. Major development was carried out on this property with installing new buildings, a jetty and fuelling pontoon. It was also used for repairs, service and maintenance of yachts. A fair number of new boats were built at this facility, including the first GRP boats that Moody built - these were the Salar 40 designed by Laurent Giles. This site was sold in 1968.

Stone Pier, Warsash, in Moody's ownership 1963-1968.
Photo from D.B.L. Imaging.

At this time there were plans to develop a marina at Swanwick. The sale of Stone Pier at Warsash, the Abbey and the petrol station would eventually assist in the finance of this ambitious and forward thinking development. Swanwick would be one of the first marinas in the country.

It can also be noted from the diagram on page 25 that letters A-G denote sites of various properties that have been owned by the Moody family - incidentally Reginald Moody owned Victory Cottages for a short period and it is believed that these were sold to assist in the financial arrangements of dissolving A.H. and F. Moody in 1932.

The Marina goes Ahead!

Phase One

With the land purchases complete and the management structure in place, design evaluation discussed, planning permission agreed, it was time now to begin the work necessary for the build of the marina. There were test borings to do, estimates for dredging, sheath piling etc. and before we knew it, Phase One had begun. By late Autumn 1967, a Dutch dredging company had moved in

Pile driver at work installing first lifting bay for new hoist during development of the marina, circa. 1967. Photo from David Moody collection.

to change the face of Lower Swanwick forever. The dredging went on 24 hours a day, land work had started, and infill had arrived by lorry from all over Hampshire.

All work was completed and the marina was ready for occupation by mid-1968. The first phase consisted of two floating piers, A and B jetties. Whilst the development of the property was going ahead, so was the expansion of the businesses. The sales department had a better base to work from, displaying boats in an attractive environment with easy access. The repair yard was able to move forward with great gusto and changed from using slipways for lifting boats to mobile motorised hoists similar to those used for moving containers. A new marina shop was built and for a time led the field in chandlery. Marina facilities improved dramatically in every quarter.

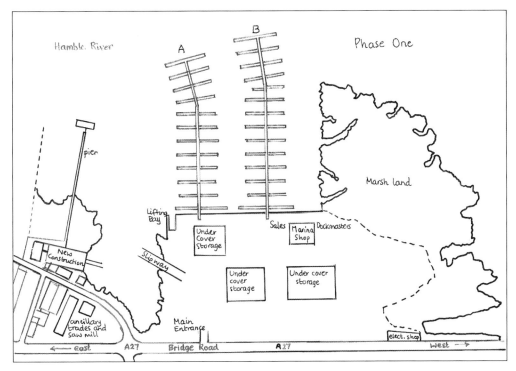

Plan to show phase one of the development of the marina and associated yard buildings mid 1968.

Phase Two

Things were now moving forward and the development of Phase Two of the Marina began towards the end of 1971. This consisted of a further three floating piers to the west of the original Phase One. These were D, E and F jetties. The dredger moved in and, to meet deadlines and to minimise the inconvenience to the local residents, worked around the clock once again. Huge barges reappeared to move up and down the river to coincide with tides so that the mud that had been removed by the dredgers could be disposed of in deep water beyond the Isle of Wight. Land was reclaimed and the steel sheath piling had to be driven in by large, noisy pile drivers to retain the reclaimed land.

You will note that the creek that had been the life of the Company for many years had now been filled in and the Bunny had been piped to its new outfall. The dock to the west of the yard was also in-filled.

From a business point of view, the dry storage of boats had increased dramatically, another hoist had been purchased and the sheds that had been so important to us during the late 30s and Second World War had now been demolished. New facilities had to be built to cater for the increase in marina population.

Aerial photograph of the Marina taken from the east late 70s early 80s. Photo from D.B.L. Imaging.

Swanwick Marina as it was in 2005. Photo from David Moody collection.

Phase Three

This consisted of one floating pier (A jetty) which was constructed in 1979 to the east of Phase One. Again services in all areas continued to improve with the increase of marina population. Yet another hoist was purchased, new building shops were erected to cater for the ever increasing demand for the Moody product during the 1970s and early 80s. A final floating pier (X jetty) was installed between the existing marina and the public hard. At this time we were at the end of our planning. Any further enlargement would probably not have been viable or acceptable to the planners. Work continued on improving the site by installing a second lift bay enabling us to lift up to 65 tons. The open ended sheds in the centre of the yard were demolished and the original sheds on *sector 7* were re-clad. New dockmaster offices and toilets were installed and the entrance to the marina had been moved to coincide with the new entrance to Swanwick Lane. Traffic lights were eventually installed to manage the sheer weight of traffic on the A27. Car Parks were covered in asphalt and facilities were improving continuously. From our very humble beginnings, we had become a multi-million pound business, covering all areas of the boating industry, known the world over.

This photograph shows Dame Ellen MacArthur's yacht "Kingfisher" being prepared for her transportation to the London International Boat Show following her epic round the world single-handed voyage. Kingfisher has been lifted by a Wise boat lifter which has a capacity of 65 tons. There were two other smaller machines of less lifting capacity.

How times have changed. The photograph on the right shows a yacht ready for launching. Boats in those early days had to be moved on greased ways with block and tackle. This was prior to the creek being filled in.

This yacht is now waiting for the tide to rise so it may be floated off. Coincidently, this yacht is in the same area where Kingfisher was standing, mentioned above.

The plan below is a rough indication of the positioning of the buildings in 2005. The open spaces were either used for yacht storage or car parking.

Dame Ellen MacArthur's yacht Kingfisher at Swanwick. Photo from David Moody collection.

A Dr Harrison-Butler design waiting to be floated on a high tide, circa. 1930s.
Photo from Joan Jardine-Brown collection.

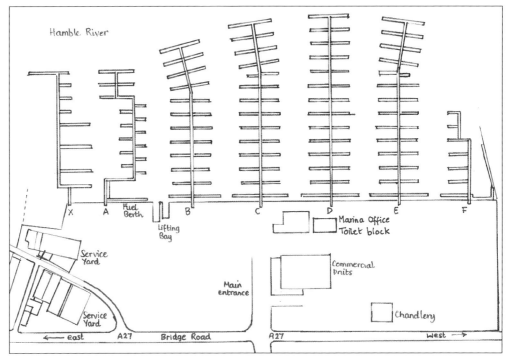

Plan of Marina and buildings, 2005.

The Timber Yachts

Photographs and more detail on a selection of private yachts built through the years, can be seen on page 63 onwards, starting with Vindilis in April 1935. The detail comes from a variety of sources. Any owners, where mentioned, would be the individuals who contracted the build of the boat.

The specification and detail have been taken from original sales literature and specification sheets published at the time. You will notice that some of the language is quite different to the terminology used today! There seem to be many favourite phrases. Most boats had "ample cupboard space" and had "quite pleasing lines". The doghouses were almost always "useful"! Racing boats were without exception "quite fast". Electric starting and lighting throughout was phased in with great excitement. The photographs also pick out the skippers clad in gleaming white overalls. Standards were obviously held at a premium.

In the early days of boatbuilding at Swanwick, timber had to be sourced. The main supplier was Houghtons at Durley - a major saw mill and timber supplier for the area. My father recalls that both Eddy Bunday and my Grandfather, Reginald, used to travel to Houghtons in a horse drawn cart with all the templates. To give a yacht maximum strength at this stage, they always tried to match the shape of the template to the grain of the piece of timber which gave much more strength, but there was, unfortunately, a lot of wastage with this system. The timber used in those early days was invariably English oak. When a perfect match for a knee or a stem was found, avoiding all sap and heart wood, this was quite an achievement and Mr Bunday and Reginald used to wax lyrical!

The diagram shows how a template of a knee would be laid on a plank of timber to maximise its strength with the formation of the grain.

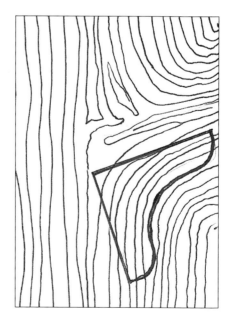

Following the selection of the timber, it was marked and then always delivered on a Saturday morning in a six horse drawn cart with a separate lifting apparatus. As you can imagine, the bulks of timber were large and very heavy. The timber was dropped off at the end of Swanwick Lane and then taken to a manually operated pit saw where a template was laid on again and marked. The timber was rough sawn and finished with a carpenter's adze and hand plane. As time passed and glues improved laminates were more common.

The drawing shows the placing of a template over a piece of timber with ideal grain pattern prior to cutting.

As a general rule of thumb, it would appear that those early boats were built for £100 to £135 per ton and by the early 60s this had crept to around £1,000 per ton and £2,000 per ton by the early to mid 70s. You can see that those boats were a good investment. Generally, boats of this standard, and providing they were well maintained, increased in value over the years, apart from times of recession and hostilities. This continued to be the case for yachts built up until the early to mid 1990s when yachts seemed to lose value from the date of purchase. This was probably due to lower inflation and supply keeping up with demand, due to improved technology which was not the case in earlier times. There will always be exceptions to this.

On the following photographs, later in the book, it should be noted that a number of the boats had upturned wooden dinghies on deck. These were also built by the company and would have cost approximately £25. Generally, it would have been the apprentices' job to build the dinghies.

In the early 1930s there was a reluctance to move into manufacturing and I think it is important to understand how the process changed over the years in the purchase of boats. Originally you had a number of naval architects - without doubt professional people - whom customers used to consult for a design, and then the architect would locate and choose the best builder for the purpose. Generally, the naval architect would draw up the contract and agree the price to be paid. Therefore, there was little scope at this time for the manufacturer to make a reasonable profit which is so important for business expansion. When everything was finalised, the contract would be signed between the builder and the purchaser with an agreed completion date. It would appear that in those early days the terms of payment would be:

- The sum of "one fourth" with order,
- A further sum of "one fourth" when the yacht is in frame.
- A further sum of "one fourth" when the yacht is completely planked and decks are laid.
- A final payment of "one fourth" when the yacht is complete in all respects and in accordance with the plans and specification before being referred to and following satisfactory sea trials.

As time passed practices changed and the manufacturer became more involved with the contracts, and producing a boat became more of a three way co-operation between designer, builder and customer. Today by contrast with production boats, the builder buys the design and sells the boat to the customer, either directly or through distributors.

On this point, I would like to share with you copies of several letters between John Laurent Giles and Moodys in the mid 1930s confirming the specification of a new yacht, to be named Andrillot,

I hope that this gives a picture of how business practices have developed over the years and how buying a boat is accessible to far more people of different walks of life as building methods and materials have changed. Finally with the improvements of travel and communications, the business had become global.

LAURENT GILES & PARTNERS,

4, QUAY HILL, LYMINGTON, HAMPSHIRE.

YACHT ARCHITECTS
AND
OWNERS' AGENTS.

TELEPHONE Nº6.
TELEGRAMS LYMINGTON 6.

Messrs. Moody & Sons,

6th
March,
1935

Dear Sirs,

25' 0" O.A. Yacht for
R. Kinnersley Esq

We enclose herewith:-

1. Print General Arrangement Sketch Plan of 25-ft. o.a. yacht.

2. Specification 23'3" o.a. yacht and small scale lines.

The proposed 25-ft. yacht will follow generally the specification and lines of the 23-ft. yacht; scantlings proportionately increased; pitch pine planking in place of oregon and teak, bright work in place of mahogany; ballast keel 30 cwts, and fittings and equipment proportionately increased in size.

The yacht to be arranged as shown on General Arrangement plan with:

Cockpit: Teak seats on either hand and at fore-end, teak skirting and caulked floor.

Cabin: Teak companion ladder; to starboard, oil skin locker; Galley arranged with Taylors' 'Paraffin' stove number 029, and elm folding side-table

-1-

Messrs. Moody & Sons.   6th March, 1935.

Cabin - contd: (fitted card table hinges)
               locker and pantry over,
lockers beneath.

To Port: Settee with 2½" Dunlop or other
mattress covered leather cloth, locker in
after bulkhead.

Forward: Two bunks, each with 2½" Dunlop
furniture mattresses. To be
of pine, painted generally.

We should be pleased to receive your tender
for the construction of this yacht.   It is
understood that you will have the opportunity
to revise your tender, should be necessary, on
production of the final plans and specification
before signing contract.

          Yours faithfully,

          LAURENT GILES & PARTNERS.

ENC;

LAURENT GILES & PARTNERS,

4. QUAY HILL, LYMINGTON,
HAMPSHIRE.

YACHT ARCHITECTS
AND
OWNERS' AGENTS.

TELEPHONE Nº 6.
TELEGRAMS LYMINGTON 6.

Messrs. Moody & Son   9th April,
     Boat Builders,   1935
        SWANWICK SHORE.
          Nr. Southampton.

Dear Sirs,
          Yacht for R. Kinnersley.

     We are forwarding Agreement and Speci-
fication under separate cover.

     The Specification keeps to your proposal
except that mast is to be cut from log of
silver spruce or oregon pine and to be entirely
free from knots, and as follows:

Binnacle ("MEDWAY").............£4. 10. 0 gross

Galley stove (Taylors' "Para-fin"
      No. 029)...................5. 17. 6   "

Saloon lamp, say.................1. 0. 0

Additional sails, say............7. 10. 0

Sundries, say.....................1. 2. 6

Total additions, say..............   £20. 0. 0

Allowances:

Windlass, say....................3. 0. 0

Roller reefing, say..............2. 0. 0
                              5. 0. 0

                            £15. 0. 0

Quoted, 27th March...............   295. 0. 0

Contract Price...................   £310. 0. 0

Messrs. Moody & Son,   9th April, 1925

-2-

        We trust this will meet with your approval
and confirmation.

                    Yours faithfully:

                    LAURENT GILES & PARTNERS.

LAURENT GILES & PARTNERS,

4, QUAY HILL, LYMINGTON, HAMPSHIRE.

YACHT ARCHITECTS
AND
OWNERS' AGENTS.

TELEPHONE Nº 6.
TELEGRAMS LYMINGTON 6.

Messrs. Moody & Son,   7th June,
Boat Builders,   1935
BURSLEDON.

Dear Sir,   R. Kinnersley Esq.

   We are forwarding by this post construction
plan and Sail plan of yacht for Mr. Kinnersley
and beg to enclose 10% deposit on Purchase
price herewith, the remainder of the first
instalment on laying of keel.   Offsets will
be forwarded as soon as you are ready to receive
them.

        Please note that Mr. Kinnersley has
now asked us for the gaff sail plan.   We
should be pleased if you will compare this
with the original sail plan, also forwarded
to you, and inform us of any possible additional
cost.

                     Yours faithfully,

                     LAURENT GILES & PARTNERS.

SPECIFICATION FOR A 25-FT. O.A. DAY CRUISER

```
L.O.A................25.00 feet
Des. W.L.............21.50    "
Beam (Extreme)....... 7.10    "
Draft................ 4.50    "
Ballast Keel (iron)..
```

1. GENERAL:

The Yacht is to be simply but well constructed
in all respects to the satisfaction of the
Architects.   The hull is to be accurately built
to the form given in the Table of Offsets.
The lines of the Yacht are to be laid down full
size in the mould loft and carefully faired.
During construction great care to be taken that
the form of the Yacht is accurately maintained
in all respects, and that all curves and lines
are perfectly fair and eyesweet.
Sheer line to be set off after removal of shores.
All timber employed in the construction of the
Yacht to be of good quality and free from knots,
shakes and sapwood.

-:-:-:-:-:-

The Moody Family at War 1939-1945

With the 1930s coming to a close, it was clear that Britain would be plunged into war and the company would be in a position to play an active, practical part in the war effort. Meetings took place with the Fairmile Company to discuss whether the partially prefabricated motor launch and MTBs could be constructed at Swanwick. It was decided that as our workforce was skilled, a more technical role was plausible and the company undertook to build the 72ft Harbour Defence Motor Launch (HDML) and many other smaller craft mentioned in my list on page 157. Prior to the outbreak of hostilities in Europe there was a skilled labour force available to carry out this work, but there seemed to be a delay before the contracts were awarded.

With the confirmation of the contracts, it was full steam ahead and over 123 assorted timber vessels were built for the Admiralty at Swanwick during the war years. On top of this there were a number of whalers and dinghies which have not been officially recorded. Admiralty numbering was generally made up of the first two digits being the year of order and the last three or four digits were the identification numbers given to the vessel. For example, 37290 would mean ordered in 1937 and 290 was the identification number. Where possible, all information available has been given in the itemised list.

It is understood that the company was employing approximately 200 people at this time. You can imagine, to support this volume of work, the ordering and supply of materials was equally important. My father recalls that during most weeks there were two deliveries of timber, mainly from Williams Timber Merchants from London. This would have been mostly African mahogany. He also recalls major deliveries from Simpson and Lawrence of Scotland who supplied many of the stem head fittings, stanchion and stanchion bases, anchors and chain, windlass and fairleads. The engine suppliers were Gardner, Ford Parsons and Perkins, among others.

The HDML was of double diagonal construction with the first skin being put in place and then a layer of calico canvas and white lead followed by an opposing plank. These planks were fastened approximately every five inch centres. Having been involved as an apprentice in the build of a Thames Conservancy launch, I can relate to how difficult it must have been for the person holding the 'dolly' whilst the rivets were being hammered into shape. As the rivet tightened, white lead would come oozing out of the plank joints and mainly onto the person holding the dolly as you were working under the vessel, lying on your back. There was no escape. You went home filthy.

Moody were also commissioned by the Admiralty to carry out many repairs and maintenance on craft that not only originated from Swanwick, but those that were in active service within the area. It was also found in some cases that some of the landing craft had to have their bottoms reinforcing. My Uncle Alan recalled in his book, "Boatbuilding on the Hamble River", that the morning after the Dieppe raid the creek, now infilled, was full of landing craft. They had been badly damaged by enemy fire and left there for repair. They were found to still have had on board, active hand grenades and ammunition and loaded guns. Many men had been killed. A short time before D-Day the company had been briefed that heavy losses and damage would be likely on the invasion. The company was to carry many spares in readiness for every eventuality.

Over the course of the war, the company had played a very important part in building Admiralty craft. In assisting to keep the existing small craft fleet in action, in excess of 2,000 vessels of all types had been repaired and refitted at Swanwick. On information available, it would appear that the workforce had worked extremely long hours but morale was said to have been high throughout these difficult times. After a day's work, the employees took on other roles in the evening - Home Guard and fire watching etc. Everyone was keen to play their part in the war effort as fully as possible.

WORLD SHIP SOCIETY

SMALL CRAFT GROUP

With all the pleasure yachts built by the company now listed, I had no record of the war-built military boats. Alan Watson of the Medusa Trust suggested I contacted Philip Simons of the World Ship Society - Small Craft Group (SCG), a group of historians, authors and enthusiasts engaged in the study of military small craft, Philip, together with Terry Holtham, the editor of the Group journal, were able to put together from their records, a comprehensive list of military craft built by Moody during and after World War II.

The aims of the SCG:

- To research the development and individual histories of small craft past and present.

- To identify and record craft that have been disposed of into private or commercial ownership.

- Collect and establish a photographic library of craft past and present, both in service and post service condition

- To collate all available information and create lists of small craft by type, class, service and record names, numbers, dimensions, builders and fates.

- To produce and maintain a register of surviving craft by type or class, in order to help owners of ex-military craft to identify their vessels.

The group publishes books on all aspects of the subject and these include their most recent works "HM Customs and Excise Cutters and Launches" by Philip Simons and "Crash Boats - 63ft Aircraft Rescue Boat - Part One" by David Linley and Terry Holtham. If you would like to contact the group, please send your enquiry to Anthony Holtham, 5 Rogate Drive.Thornbury, Plymouth PL6 8SY.

Ring the Changes

From Wood to GRP

The next significant page in our history came with the decision to test the market with a new product called Glass Reinforced Plastic (GRP). You can imagine the resistance from the traditionalist and from the qualified craftsmen!

I suppose they could see this as a threat, but the time was right with more people having more leisure time and making more money. The market was expanding, therefore technology and research and development had to move forward to cater for this. Moody were at the forefront of this movement. With the decisions made, it was decided to move forward in a balanced way.

I have already mentioned that at that time we owned the yard at Warsash-the former-HMS Tormentor. This was to be the venue of our first venture into fitting out glass fibre boats. We had decided not to begin moulding our own boats until a later date because of the investment that would have been needed to set up a new plant for moulding. The Salar 40 had been designed by Laurent Giles & Partners circa 1966 for Salterns Yacht Agency. Moody were to build the first one in timber at their Swanwick yard in 1966. This was called Salmo Salar and was owned by Air Vice Marshall E. L. Colbeck Welsh CB OBE DFC RAF. This was to be used as the plug to make the mould. The glass fibre engineering was to be done by Kemp and Pitt Ltd. A second yacht was to be built in timber later that year, named Dorcelle, owned by Mr D. W. Morrell. A further five were to be moulded

Photos above and below: Halberdier 36 mouldings ready for fit-out, circa. 1968 at Swanwick. Photo from David Moody collection.

by Kemp and Pitt and fitted out by Moody at our Warsash yard. These were Delfen Sailor, Lady Kate, Gander, Serifa, and Sinbad the Salar. Our contract to build the Salar 40 then expired.

In parallel with this, Moody and Marine Construction were developing their own 36ft motorsailer to an Alan Hill design. This was the Halberdier 36 which won two prestigious awards as Boat of the Show, one year at London and runner up another year. She was a true motor sailer with a deep centre cockpit and wheel house over. She was available in sloop or ketch forms, although ketch was the most popular. The accommodation included an aft cabin which was accessible from the cockpit. Twenty nine of these craft were eventually sold. We also developed an aft cockpit deck saloon model on the same hull called a Cavalier 36. Eight of these were built. The mouldings were engineered by Marine Construction.

A further boat was developed with Marine Construction Ltd. - the Carbineer 44 - to a Laurent Giles design. She was later extended to 46ft by means of slightly straightening the stem and extending the transom. Also at this time we had encapsulated the keel in fibre glass. Prior to this the keels had been bolted on similar to a wooden boat. We were to build 32 Carbineers between 1969 and 1978.

Photo from David Moody collection.

Carbineer 44 mouldings being delivered to Swanwick, circa. 1969. Photo from David Moody collection.

Whilst the numbers of these boats built and sold do not reflect the number sold today, it was still production boatbuilding in its infancy. Both these models will take their place in marine history as being modern day classics. They are sought after today.

The photograph shows the Carbineer 44 on a low loader with Eric White third from the left. Eric was the Managing Director of Marine Construction.

In those early days the industry had thought it had found the perfect material and indeed with technology and science the resins have been dramatically improved over time. In the early years it did not come without its problems that had to be addressed - generally on resale following surveys. Once identified, and the sometimes costly remedial work being carried out to the correct specification, it did not appear to affect the residual value although sometimes a stigma attached itself to the boat.

Surveyors identified "wicking" which was water passing through the gel coat and being absorbed into the fibreglass fibres and would appear raised on what should be shiny bottom. This problem would worsen into blisters and when lanced would reveal a strong smell resembling vinegar. It was often referred to as "osmosis". This is a very non-scientific explanation and I think was due to the gel coats of their day not being completely water tight or bad attention when laying up the boat. I am sure I have not covered all the reasons why this would happen. It was also essential to keep your bilges dry to stop water ingress from the inside of the boat. As I have said before, technology and science move forward and most of these early problems have been eradicated.

Following the Carbineer, there were a number of other designs that Moody fitted out, but always the hull and superstructure was moulded by specialists.

• Lancer 42	moulded by Tyler Boat Company	5 built
• Moody 44	moulded by Halmatic Ltd.	18 built
• Moody 42	moulded by Robert Ives Boatbuilding Ltd.	54 built
• Grenadier 134	moulded by Robert Ives Boatbuilding Ltd.	10 built
• Grenadier 119	moulded by Robert Ives Boatbuilding Ltd.	3 built
• Moody 52	moulded by Halmatic Ltd	7 built

This is a few of the production boats which we built at Swanwick and were classed as "semi-custom built". The craftsmanship in the fit out of all these boats was not compromised. They were all built to the highest standards and many were built to Lloyds supervision. These standards were maintained, reflecting the stance my Great Grandfather took in 1935. The Moody 47 was the first boat to be moulded and fitted out by Moody at Swanwick. There were 22 built.

The Moody Group

Prior to the Company becoming involved in building private yachts, I have already outlined that it concentrated on repairs, maintenance and service of yachts that were in the yard and on the river and this was complemented with the build of small craft such as dinghies. From 1935, the service facility continued in parallel with the boatbuilding and took on some major refits even during hostilities in the Second World War. Repairs to Admiralty craft totalled over 2,000.

Inside the Moody chandlery - one of the first of its type in the country. Photo from D.B.L. Imaging.

The service side of the yard continued to be very important in recent years. The sale of new boats generated work once they had been handed over to the customer. There was invariably warranty work to be attended to and boat owners might have often required some electronics or extras fitted. The spin off from new boat sales to the repair yard became increasingly valuable to them. Nothing was too small a job for the repair yard - they even became involved in fitting out some larger yachts which did not compete with our own sales operation.

To the irritation of some of our customers in the late 80s, we decided to separate the businesses so as to keep a tighter financial control over their activities. In 1987 it was agreed that A.H. Moody & Son would be the holding company having responsibility for the marina and chandlery and any leases to marine related businesses hiring premises from us.

The photograph (above) shows the interior of the chandlery in the early 80s. It was Gordon's responsibility initially to oversee this reorganisation as he remained Chairman and Managing Director of the parent company. My brother John took over as Chairman when Gordon retired and my cousin Graham took the role of Managing Director.

As the building of new yachts at Swanwick was being phased out, more emphasis was being placed on the development of the buildings to be leased out, therefore playing more of a landlord role. The sales and marketing side of the business from then became Moody Marketing and Development Ltd, and later Moody Yachts International Ltd. with John the Managing Director. When he became Chairman of the Group, I became Managing Director of the sales operation. The responsibility of this business was to maintain the sales, research and development of the Moody brand and to support any dealerships

6 Fairline 50s in the sales pen at Swanwick newly owned or awaiting handover, circa 1980s. Photo by Tony Willey.

that we held. At this time, we were representing Fairline, and under the umbrella of Solent Powerboats Ltd, the Princess range. In addition we had a thriving Used Boat Sales department and an Insurance department, primarily set up to provide a service to Moody owners.

Aztec Lady partially fitted out by the repair yard, seen here sailing mid-70s. Photo from D.B.L. Imaging.

I was at this time heavily involved with the powerboat sales and found this an exciting experience. The clientele buying powerboats was quite different to those who bought sailboats. For a time we were very successful in this market. The repair yard became Graham Moody's responsibility and this business was called A.H.M. (Service and Construction) Ltd, and later Moody (Service and Construction) Ltd.

He was the Managing Director. This company's focus was the development and construction of yachts built at Swanwick - refits, repairs, boat lifting and storage.

The photograph opposite is Aztec Lady. This hull and superstructure was built by Joyce Marine of Southampton. She laid unfinished in a mud berth in Southampton for a number of years before being purchased by her late owner who brought her to Swanwick where the repair yard assisted in the fit out. The repair yard was well placed to take on this type of contract.

The photograph below shows the Maxi-rater Drum being launched and rigged with many people looking on. In 1988 new construction at Swanwick was being phased out with more emphasis being placed on repairs and maintenance of private yachts. Later, another responsibility of this part of the company was the manufacture of teak laid decks for production yachts and motor yachts. These were manufactured on a jig off the boat and then fitted at a later date. This was proving to be very successful with a number of major manufacturers using this system. Whilst Moodys were mainly known for the building of many quality timber and GRP yachts, the supply of many hundreds of yachts jointly developed with Marine Projects and the other activities based at Swanwick were also of significant importance. This contributed to the uniqueness of A.H. Moody & Son Ltd.

Drum having her mast stepped following repairs. She successfully competed in the 1985/86 Whitbread Round the World yacht race, scoring 3rd overall. Photo by Tony Willey.

The Public Face of Moodys

I have already spoken briefly of the Bursledon Regatta and Fair. This was hosted by us for many years and was the highlight of the year, taking place in the early Autumn. Its popularity ebbed and flowed over the years, but still takes place today at a slightly different venue due to the development of the marina. It is a fantastic traditional event and we all have fond memories of this. The committee boat, an old Admiralty drifter which served as our derrick boat was moored off the end of the public hard in Swanwick Shore

The Q class was a popular one design of the time. Seen here racing at Bursledon Regatta. Photo from Elizabeth Jowett.

Road - right outside Myrtle Cottage. The programme would begin with many dinghy and keelboat races in the morning and go through the afternoon with rowing, swimming, canoeing and outboard races. It generally ended with a water carnival, which was always great fun. There was a fairground in the field opposite the yard and it all came to a grand finale around nine o'clock with a firework display.

The sale of boats did not happen without investment. We exhibited at the very first London Boat Show in 1953. The show outgrew its first venue of Olympia and moved to Earls Court. More recently it moved to Excel in London's Dockland. Every year Moodys was well represented. We always had a major stand in a prominent position and were one of the few long standing exhibitors at this event. We also exhibited at Southampton from inauguration. Southampton was a vital show to the industry at the right time of year. We preferred it as we could live at home and usually the weather was kind to us. In addition to this, we also exhibited in many European boat shows.

Mr Alan Moody OBE receiving the Queen's Award for Export Achievement from the Lord Lieutenant of Hampshire, 1978. Photo from David Moody collection.

One of the greatest moments in the history of the company was to be awarded the Queen's Award for Export Achievement on 21 April 1978. In the photograph my Uncle Alan is receiving this award on behalf of the company from the Lord Lieutenant of Hampshire, the Earl of Malmesbury. It was a truly memorable day with many activities and festivities to mark the occasion.

Sail past following a very successful Moody Midsummer Meet 1993.
Photo by Tony Willey.

The London show introduced the 'Boat of the Show' award for a short period and we were honoured to receive this in 1965 for Firedancer owned by D. S. Cortell. In 1967 we received third prize for the Halberdier 36 - Mirabelle II - owned by Dr. J. B. Shield. Finally in 1968 we received the Boat of the Show award for the Halberdier 36, Bellrock II, owned by Mr Passmore. We received two Lloyds Trophy Awards for the best yacht built to Lloyds classification. These were for the yachts Martinus - owned by Mr J.R.P. Martin, and Larne owned by Mr Marryat. The business, from its humble beginnings had become a truly international company with a global reputation.

In the late 70s, the idea of a Used Boat Show was taken to the organisers of the Southampton show - then Artman and Partners. With discussions and agreement reached, the show was staged at Swanwick and Hamble to coincide with the Southampton show. What great foresight of the then organisers of the show. It became an event in its own right and very important to Moodys. At its peak, it attracted some 16,000 visitors, selling more than 60 used boats of all sizes. Moody eventually 'went it alone' and it still exists today.

In 1981 the Moody Owners' Association was formed by founder members Topsy and Geoffrey Godfrey. This organised many social events for like-minded people who loved their Moody yachts. They attended rendezvous, meetings, parties etc. There were also three rather spectacular 'Moody Midsummer Meets' which were staged at Swanwick in 1993, 1995 and 1997. A grand marquee was erected and events lasted over three days. The Princess Royal attended the Meet in 1997 to open the commemoration of 25 years continuous co-operation between Moody and Marine Projects (Plymouth) Ltd.

This is to certify that

Jonathan Moody

balanced out on a Moody yacht
on the first Diabetes Sailing Day
held by
Moody Marketing & Development Ltd
in conjunction with
Southampton General Hospital Diabetes Clinic
on 1st June 2000

Certificate given to all the children who participated in the Diabetes Day 2000.

The company also participated in various industry campaigns like - "Try a Boat" and "Go-Boating weekend". All the demonstrators were lined up and salesmen's leave cancelled and the non boating public were invited to 'Have a go!' This took place over two days and literally thousands of people were given the chance to go boating free of charge. This was a tremendous achievement with so many branches of the industry working together to achieve one goal - promoting the sport.

On a personal note, the company supported my own family in 2000. Our youngest son was diagnosed as having type-one diabetes the previous year at the age of 12. This hit us hard and we had tremendous support from the Southampton Diabetes Clinic at that time. We wanted to show our appreciation and a sailing day was organised.

We took out six boats with about forty children from the clinic with medical staff to help, crew and support. They enjoyed a mock helicopter rescue, lunch at Ocean Village and supper at the marina which was attended by local MP John Denham who was then Junior Health Minister. They really did have a great day. The sales team and friends really made the day memorable by entering into the spirit and not one of the children wound up in hospital at the end of the day. We counted them out and we counted them back!

All the family attended many boat shows both at London and Southampton. I have worked out that I, personally, have spent over two years of my life at London and

Southampton shows, plus those I have attended overseas. The photograph (left) shows the London Boat Show 1992 at Earls Court with the Moody 44, 38, 35, 336 and the Eclipse 33 being exhibited. The photograph below shows our stand at the Southampton Boat Show 1997 at Mayflower Park with the Moody 40, 36, S31 and S38 being exhibited. The company exhibited at both of these shows from the very start without a break. They were a vital tool to the success of our business. The importance of the show changed over the years. Initially it was a pure showcase, in latter years it was the place the company secured orders for the coming seasons.

The Moody stand at the London International Boat Show 1992. Photo by Tony Willey.

Moody stand at Southampton Boat Show Mayflower Park 1997. Photo by Tony Willey.

Moody Midsummer Meet, 16th - 20th June 1993

The grand marquee at the east end of the boatyard which accommodated many official functions held at the Moody Meet, June 1993. Photo by Tony Willey.

Moody's 21st Anniversary Celebrations

Twenty one years of continuous co-operation between Marine Projects (Plymouth) Ltd. and Moody.

The Mayor of Fareham opening the Moody Meet and unveiling an original sail plan of the Moody 33. Photo by Tony Willey.

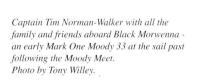
Captain Tim Norman-Walker with all the family and friends aboard Black Morwenna - an early Mark One Moody 33 at the sail past following the Moody Meet. Photo by Tony Willey.

The Diabetes Sailing Day, 1st June 2000

Coastguard helicopter from Lee-on-Solent carrying out mock exercise lifting a pretend injured person from the decks of the Moody 54. The RNLI lifeboat from Calshot was also in attendance. Photo by Tony Willey.

Group aboard Moody 54. Photo by Tony Willey.

All the children, NHS staff and Moody personnel who took part in the Diabetes Day, June 2000. Photo by Tony Willey.

The Awards

1 *London International Boat Show 1965*
Boat of the Show Award - Firedancer

2 *London International Boat Show 1967*
Boat of the Show Award Halberdier 36, Mirabelle II

3 *London International Boat Show 1968*
Boat of the Show Award Halberdier 36, Bellrock II

4 *British Nautical Awards*
Sailboat of the Year Offshore - Moody 54 Winner 2000

Moody & Marine Projects

When my brother John returned from America having worked with the Dick Bertram Corporation, he was very sales and marketing orientated and was always looking for new directions. In the late 60s, a chance meeting between David King of Marine Projects (Plymouth) Ltd, and John led to Moody selling the Princess range of motor yachts. David and two associates had the foresight to produce early production boats in GRP that proved good value for money. This was to become a huge success story. Marine Projects were purely manufacturers and only sold to selected dealers throughout the world. They later became Princess Yachts International Plc. Throughout the cooperation between Moody and Marine Projects, the services of only two naval architects were to be used - Angus Primrose and Bill Dixon. The next few pages are a tribute to their designs.

It was in 1973 that a fuel crisis in the Middle East hit the UK and fuel coupons had been issued in readiness. This could have had a major effect on powerboat sales. It was at this point that David King and John put together a joint development programme to

David King, Managing Director of Marine Projects addressing guests at the London International Boat Show Earls Court, January 1998. Photo by Tony Willey.

John Moody at the London Boat Show, 1998. Photo by Tony Willey.

produce a range of sailing yachts using the same philosophy as David had used on the power boats. This cooperation proved most successful for both companies and at its peak, nearly 400 sailing yachts were being produced each year.

This cooperation would go on for just over three decades producing 39 models and 4,233 boats being built ranging from 27ft to 64ft. The collaboration between the two companies and the manufacturing at Swanwick, resulted in Moody receiving the Queens Award for Industry in 1978 for Export Achievement. These years were times of change, excitement and reward for Britain and the industry had to adapt to this change to benefit. With the sailboat market declining in the UK, the difficult decision to dissolve this relationship was taken in 2003.

Following this decision, we were faced with no one building the Moody product. Manufacturing at Swanwick was no longer an option and another manufacturer had to be found as the sale of Moody yachts was core to our business. After a number of meetings with prospective manufacturers, we were directed towards VT Halmatic Ltd. We had worked with Halmatic in the past. An agreement was reached and a decision to develop a new product range was made.

The development team – Taken aboard the Moody 38 at the Southampton Boat Show in the mid 90s.

Left to right, designer Bill Dixon, Simon Limb Marine Projects, John Moody Managing Director Moodys, David King Managing Director Marine Projects and David Moody. Photo by Tony Willey.

The two photographs overleaf show David King and John Moody celebrating 25 years of relations between the two companies. We held a party on our stand at Earls Court in 1998 where suppliers and owners shared in the celebrations. This unique business arrangement had been the envy of many within the industry and worked well for both companies during both good and difficult times. This was an historical achievement in its own right and had been partly responsible for making the sport of sailing accessible to more people.

The Designers

Moodys and their customers consulted a number of marine naval architects over the years and the first yacht to be produced by Moody was Vindilis, which was built for the designer, Dr. T. Harrison-Butler (THB). Three further designs from his drawing board were to follow. These can be seen in the build list on page 156. We were also to build a number of yachts from the drawing board of Frederick Shepherd of Piccadilly. These 6 designs were mainly built prior to the outbreak of war in 1939, although the sister ship to Amokura, Galamara, was built later.

John Laurent Giles RDI MRINA standing at the door of this famous address 4 Quay Hill, Lymington. Note the bandage on his left index finger - an injury caused by a paper cut. Photo from Laurent Giles, Naval Architects.

Laurent Giles and Partners Ltd

There were a great number of designs from the design office of Laurent Giles and Partners Ltd. built by Moody, and the earliest boat was Andrillot, built in 1936 from the hand of John Laurent Giles. This boat was to become the forerunner to the world famous Vertue class, which is now legendary. Other classic designs, some of which were built by Moody, were the Channel class and the Brittany class. Later designs for Moody included the Carbineer 44, Moody 44, Moody 63 and Grenadier range. All were built in GRP.

Laurent Giles and Partners' offices were at number 4, Quay Hill, Lymington. As Laurent Giles and Partners changed over the years, the yachts managed to keep their distinct design identity. Moodys built many Laurent Giles designs over several decades in timber, GRP, aluminium and steel. It is my view that this company is one of the most professional and respected design offices to work with and they have designed for Moodys many yachts that will go down as classics. It is interesting that we were building boats to Laurent Giles and Partners designs from the 30s till the late 80s at Swanwick. They are still in business today and remain an International company.

Frederick R. Parker *MRINA*

Fred Parker's design office was originally at Sarisbury Green and later at Warsash. He became our favoured naval architect during the 50s and 60s and designed more than 30 individually designed yachts that were built at Swanwick. The majority of these were of timber construction. These one-off designs included ocean racing yachts, motor sailers and fast cruising yachts. These were in addition to a number of motor yachts. Fred Parker, in his day, was also known for a number of superyachts. Fred was to design Swan Dancer - the last wooden boat to be built at Swanwick, in 1970. The photograph shows Fred Parker in the centre and Gordon Moody to his left at the launch of one of his designs, Majala in April 1963.

Fred Parker, centre, attending the launching of Majala, 1963. Photo from David Moody collection.

Lt.Col.HG (Blondie) Haslar DSO OBE (left) on board Demon of Hamble with Angus Primrose inspecting the Haslar wind vane self steering gear. Photo from Ajaxnetphoto.com.

Angus Primrose

Those of us who knew Angus counted him to be one of those larger than life characters who enjoyed life and sailing. Whilst he had only designed the Moody 42 for Moodys at Swanwick, he had already designed a number of Moody boats which were being built by Marine Projects at Plymouth. This included among others the Moody 33 Mark I and Mark II, 33S and 333, all using the same hull. There were 494 boats built to this design, spanning a build duration in total of ten years from September 1973 until August 1983. This was one of the most successful in build numbers to bear the Moody name.

Angus was loaned his first Moody 33, Demon Demo, which doubled up as the company's demonstration model and also for Angus to use privately. He was to take part in the 1976 OSTAR single-handed Transatlantic race from Plymouth to Newport, Rhode Island. The start was on 5th June, but on this occasion Angus had to retire off the Azores.

Not to be beaten, Angus decided to buy his own Moody 33 called Demon of Hamble, and use it privately for cruising and to take part in many local races. He was also to enter the OSTAR Transatlantic race for a second time in 1980. This was to start on 7th June. He completed the course in 30 days 23 hours and 8 minutes and took 24th place. This was the Penduick class for craft of 32 to 44 ft.

Having successfully completed the race, Angus decided to cruise off the east coast of America and sadly in October 1980, his life was cut short when cruising off Cape Hatteras. He was caught in a freak storm and was presumed to have been swept overboard and was never found. It was a very sad loss to the yachting community. The above photograph shows Angus with Lt. Col. H.G. Blondie Hasler aboard Demon of Hamble, surveying the Hasler wind vane

Merlo Primrose launching Demon Demo with Angus, children and guests looking on. Photo from Ajaxnetphoto.com.

steering gear, which was manufactured by Gibb of Warsash. The photograph right is the launching of Demon of Hamble with Angus and his children, with Murlo his wife doing the honours of smashing the champagne over her bow. John and I can be seen hovering in the background!

Left to right: Gordon Moody, Angus Primrose and Graham Moody aboard Moody 42 Centre Cockpit discussing detail, circa. 1978. Photograph from the Southern Daily Echo.

Lt. Col H.G. "Blondie" Hasler DSO OBE., who was renowned as the leader of the famous Cockleshell Heroes of the Second World War, had himself taken part in the inaugural OSTAR Transatlanic race in 1960 and 1964 in the famous 26ft modified Folkboat with a junk rig, Jester. Blondie Hasler and Francis Chichester were pioneers of the first Transatlantic race organised by the Royal Western Yacht Club. Jester had been sold and unfortunately had to be abandoned at sea in 1988. There have a number of replicas made of this unique craft since. Blondie Hasler's second boat was called Sumner. Both Sumner and Jester were moored in the river outside Myrtle Cottage during my childhood. It is believed that Sumner is in a French museum.

Also worthy of note was David Pyle, now Director of Princess Yachts International. David took part in the 1976 OSTAR Transatlantic race in a Moody 30 called Westward. His time was 42 days 10 hours 11 minutes and he was 38th in Class J - being the Jester class up to 38ft. At this time David ran a successful yacht delivery company.

The photograph above shows Angus Primrose (centre) with Gordon Moody on his right and Graham Moody on his left, aboard one of the first Moody 42s to be built. The Moody 42 deck saloon aft cockpit and the Moody 42 CC were the most successful to be built at Swanwick with 54 of these boats being built - seven of which were the centre cockpit. Both versions were based on the same hull. The build duration of the deck saloon version was from 1977 to 1981. This included a facelift in 1980 where she became known as the Mark II. The saloon became more swept back and the bridge deck between the helm and the companionway entrance was lowered to give safer and easier access to the saloon. The centre cockpit version had a build duration of four years from 1978. The hull and deck of both models were moulded by Robert Ives Boat builders Ltd. and fitted out at Swanwick by A.H. Moody & Son Ltd. Angus had certainly made his mark in yachting circles and really played his part in another chapter of the Moody company.

Bill Dixon

Bill Dixon had already joined the offices of Angus Primrose as a naval architect when Angus was tragically lost at sea. Bill was at this time only in his early twenties. Moodys were faced with a dilemma - whether to continue to support him as a little known designer or to look elsewhere. The decision was taken to maintain the status quo and this would be seen in the future to be a good move. Bill, having come from a marine background had some good, fresh ideas and amongst his early designs were the Moody 41 and 27. These were jointly developed by Moody and Marine Projects. He became a very important member of the development team. The first boat to be designed for Moodys at Swanwick by Bill was the Moody 47 and its derivatives - the 471 and the Culverneer 500, which proved very

Bill Dixon in his design office in old Bursledon. Photo by Tony Willey.

successful. There were 31 of these boats built at Swanwick. Bill remained our favoured designer for over 20 years. He went on to become an internationally known designer of many superyachts and is currently designing and developing the new generation of Moody yachts for the current owners. One thing is for sure - Bill was always prepared to try something new.

Alan Hill

I had the pleasure of sailing with Alan Hill. Alan came from the east coast and was a very competitive sailor. Alan was responsible for designing the first GRP production boat to be built at Swanwick. This was the Halberdier 36 and later the Cavalier 36. He is an absolute character and has now taken up my favourite pastime, sailing international A-class model yachts.

Graham Moody

Our own Graham Moody worked with Fred Parker for a short time as part of his initial training and later designed two notable boats for the company - the Lancer and clinker planked Gentleman's launch. In addition to this, he did many detailed drawings on other yachts.

There were a number of other notable designers who the company worked with over the years - including Robert Clark Ltd, Sparkman and Stevens Inc., K.H. Reimers, J. Francis Jones Associates, C.R. Holman, Arthur C. Robb MBE, G.L. Watson & Co, German Frers, and probably surprisingly C.A. Nicholson and James McGruer who were competitors!

Dr. T. Harrison-Butler

I knew that the first boat that Moodys built in 1935 was Vindilis and that she was designed by Dr T Harrison-Butler. I had no idea of the fate of this boat and honestly thought that it would be very difficult to track any information down. Reality proved a rather easy journey of discovery!

Word of mouth is a marvellous thing! We were having some work done at home and I was chatting with the installer, Ron, about his sailing experiences and happened to mention the work I was doing on the archives.

Dr T. Harrison-Butler at his drawing board, circa. 1930. Photo from Joan Jardine-Brown collection.

I said that Vindilis was our first boat, shortly followed by Zingara, Lindy II and Edith Rose. Ron's ears pricked up and said that he knew exactly where Lindy II was and could put me in touch with the owner. A phone call shortly followed to the owner who then was able to give me the phone number of Joan Jardine-Brown, who was the daughter of T. Harrison-Butler, the designer of four of our early boats.

Joan was a mine of information. Approaching 90 years old, she was able to tell me details of everything in amazing clarity. The most important thing was she knew that Vindilis was lying at West Loch, near Tarbert, Scotland and in regular use. I arranged to visit Joan with my wife.

Joan's apartment was a treasure trove of yachting memorabilia and archives. She had her own library of yachting literature, all bound. She had boxes of photographs - many of them the product of an old Box Brownie number Zero. To me this was remarkable. I could take a peek into the history of her family and see the many outings taken during her life. The designer (THB as he is lovingly referred to) had handwritten his log and we were able to take this away to read and absorb and also look at photo albums which include pictures of yachts at our yard in Swanwick - some even had pictures of my father, grandfather and great grandfather.

Joan obviously was able to tell us much about THB. He was a skilled eye surgeon and held the post of Honorary Surgeon (the equivalent of a Consultant surgeon nowadays, but unpaid) in three Midlands hospitals, plus three private practices to provide an income. If that was not enough he designed yachts very successfully, as a hobby, in his spare time. For this activity he did not charge and anything he was given went to charity. Some of his designs were pirated so no one really knows how many of his yachts are in existence. It should, said Joan, go into more than a hundred.

Dr T. Harrison-Butler at the helm of Vindilis. Photo from Joan Jardine-Brown collection.

The Search for Vindilis

Following our lovely and informative day with Joan, we were armed with a wealth of information about the boats that her father had designed and we were, of course, mostly interested in the whereabouts of Moody's first private yacht that had been built in 1935 - Vindilis, built for the designer himself - Dr Harrison-Butler.

Joan had been able to put us in touch with current owner - Damon Kenneil. Damon lives with his wife, Annie, in Ardpatrick in Argyllshire. I rang Damon who was only too pleased to talk about his pride and joy! I was more than keen to view this yacht as Damon told me she was ashore at the Crinan Boatyard, close to the famous Crinan Canal and would be launched off in the next few weeks.

Owner Damon Kenneil making Vindilis ready for 2007 season at the Crinan Boatyard, Scotland. Photo from David Moody collection.

As the Highlands and Islands of Scotland are not too close to the South of England, I felt a holiday coming on! We booked to stay near Connal, just north of Oban and decided to have a week in the area and combine that with a visit to Crinan to view Vindilis.

We arranged to meet Damon whilst he was frantically working to prepare the boat for launching for the 2007 season. We found him in the shed at the Crinan Boatyard covered in dust with a welcoming smile and handshake. The photograph shows Damon hard at work. I felt somewhat emotional. The boat standing there had been built by the hands of my Great Grandfather and Grandfather and after 70 years she was still looking proud and seaworthy. This was thanks to the time and attention that had been given to her by her previous owners and in particular, Damon.

Damon told us that he had first seen Vindilis in Granton Harbour, Edinburgh in 1970 when he was a student at university. He knew then that this was the boat for him, but she was unavailable at the time. He returned to Granton in 1979 and found she was coming on the market and quickly put in an acceptable offer, subject to satisfactory survey as he knew there were other people interested. The survey proved that poor Vindilis was in a sad state and would need ongoing maintenance, but he and his family were happy to rise to the challenge. In the autumn of 1979, Damon sailed Vindilis from Granton Harbour to the Caledonian Canal at Inverness. From there he travelled through the Canal to Fort William and then sailed her down the west coast to Ardpatrick, West Loch, Tarbert. On his maiden voyage he encountered gale force winds and fog and had to make a number of unscheduled stops due to adverse weather.

Damon made many changes to make Vindilis more user friendly for single handed sailing. In 1991 he changed her rig from a yawl to a mast head cutter. He had to replace the rudder as it had warped and he also changed the shape of the rudder as he felt manoeuvrability could be improved. This was not so aesthetically pleasing, but nevertheless very functional. Also the Stuart Turner petrol engine was replaced with a 2x

View of Vindilis' cockpit. Note the side cockpit combings. This allows for good visibility forward. Photo from David Moody collection.

cylinder Yanmar 2 GM 20 diesel engine. His latest investment was the replacement of all the iron floors with new cast bronze floors of which I think Dr Harrison-Butler would have approved. Approximately 70 steam bent frames were replaced in oak and all centreline bolts were replaced in bronze and copper rod. The hood end fastenings were also replaced with bronze screws at this time. The photograph of the cockpit shows how the designer gave thought to forward visibility past the coach roof sides and many would say Damon improved this further by raising the cockpit sole above the waterline so as to make it self draining, thereby helping to maintain the integrity of the surrounding timber.

Damon admits that Vindilis is a little large for a day boat but he enjoys using her in this way. From West Loch, Tarbert, his favourite sailing area is around the picturesque north end of the Isle of Gigha which is approximately six miles from his home.

Vindilis without original rudder at Crinan Boatyard. Photo from David Moody collection.

Vindilis - Chain of Ownership
Official number 163672

Port of Registration - Southampton

- Dr. Thomas Harrison-Butler of Birmingham - designer - owner from May 1935
- Frederick Richard Hole of Bournemouth - June 1944
- Cyril John Cole of Yeovil - January 1949
- Fred Sewell Stevens of Torquay - June 1956
- Dr. Alistair Kerr James of Wiltshire - October 1957
- Damon Balfour Nelson Kenneil of Tarbert - July 1979
- Anne Janet Keith Kenneil of Tarbert - March 2006

Launching Vindilis

You might think that finding out information about a launching that took place over 70 years ago would be difficult. It could be, if we were not dealing with two families who had meticulous records and memories reaching back decades!

Joan Jardine-Brown had loaned me the log, handwritten by her father (THB), from the early days of Vindilis and also the guest book that had autographs of the parties who were on board many of the outings. One of the pages of the guest book was a list of the people who were present at the supper which was held to celebrate the launching of Vindilis that took place on 6th April 1935.

Owner and guests arriving at Swanwick to celebrate the launching of Vindilis, April 1935. Photo from Joan Jardine-Brown collection.

Information of the event was clearly found in the log and THB's own words tell us that *"it took place at 12.45 on top of the spring tide. It was a fine sunny day."* He gave details of the guests arrivals, many of whom came from some distance. He even mentioned that car troubles nearly made some guests late. "Nellie" (THB's nickname for his wife, Ellen) did the honours and christened Vindilis, not with the customary champagne, but rather with a bottle of Green's sherry, which was smashed over the stern. THB and Eddy Bunday were delighted to find that Vindilis 'floated on her lines'. Her topsides were black with a gold line. THB felt that a dark colour took away the bulkiness of the hull.

"In the evening, we gave a supper." Joan showed us the guest list and gave us the names of her personal friends who attended. The designer's signature is the last on the centre column overleaf. I looked at the remaining signatures. Most of the names were very familiar to me and I knew that they would be even more familiar to my father. Joan said that she thought the supper took place at the pub on Sarisbury Green (which we thought had been called the New Inn at that time.) I couldn't wait to talk to my father about this!

Gordon was very animated when he saw the list and almost waxed lyrical about the characters who seemed to come alive when he spoke of them. I felt another list coming on!

- A.H. Moody - my great grandfather
- Mr Beale - company clerk
- Harold Daish - engineer. *His grandson, Kit, is now my next door neighbour*
- Percy Wakeman - rigger
- Eddy Bunday - yard foreman *(Yard manager in all but name)*
- R.H. Moody - my grandfather
- Mr Ambrose - shipwright
- John Blazdale - apprentice engineer at the time
- Roy Williamson - engineer and my uncle
- E. Andrew - rigger
- H. George Sanford - painter

- Dick Edward - wheelwright, coach builder. *Worked with the shipwrights*
- Don Lush - joiner, boat builder
- Lionel Willsher - boat builder. *My boss during my apprenticeship!*
- Bill Kemish - boat builder
- John Alner - lofter, boat builder
- Robert Bundy - boat builder and brother of Eddie
- Walt Gasby - boat builder
- Andrew Matcham - rigger. *Had rented Myrtle Cottage for a time from A.H. Moody*
- Tom Allen - boat builder and spar maker
- Jimmy Read - rigger
- Bill Smart - shipwright. *Many of the Smart family worked at Moodys to date*
- William Fay - painter
- George Gregory - labourer
- B.M. Alner - joiner. Father of John
- J.N. Lane - "Laddy". Ship's joiner. Later foreman. *Attended my wedding!*
- Les Stamp - painter sign writer
- Ted Turner - shipwright
- Fred Moody - shipwright. My great, great uncle
- Dick Ellis Snr. - labourer. *His son, Dick also worked in the yard and became yard foreman in later years.*
- Harry Smith - rigger/launch man
- Charlie Bevis
- J. Bevis
- Perce Rosier - painter
- R. Button - fitter
- Bill Mitchell - architect and house joiner
- Jim Andrews - boat builder and son of rigger. *Went into the navy.*

Gordon was not sure of the venue. He consulted his elder sister, Audrey, who was adamant that it had taken place in the Parish rooms, Sarisbury Green, and could even say that "Newburys (the local shop) did the catering". A quick reference to the log confirmed that she was correct.

The Smallpiece family, friends of The Harrison-Butlers, also were present. They had owned an HB design before becoming very keen on racing. They are mentioned on a number of occasions in this book, as owners of the many Josephines. I was interested to read in the log that my great grandfather also attended this occasion despite *"having been ill with rheumatism. He turned up and sat in the middle of the high table. I sat at the other end. We had a few speeches and songs. There had not been a yard dinner for 65 years!!"* I note with amusement that A.H. did not fund this dinner either!

Original brass nameplate supplied by the builders A.H. Moody & Son Ltd., 1935.

Designers throughout history have tried to reach the best compromise using the technology and the materials available at the time to design cruising boats to give them good sailing qualities with the largest amount of usable space for accommodation. Vindilis' interior would have been regarded as spacious for her day. Today, the designers of cruising boats are still trying to push these boundaries to reach the optimum compromise.

61

Vindilis Launching Supper Guestlist

*Taken from the original visitor's book at the launching supper for Vindilis held at the Parish Rooms, Sarisbury Green.
Dr T. Harrison-Butler's signature is the last in the central column.*

The following selection of craft illustrates the earliest timber yachts built by Moody at Swanwick.

Vindilis

LOA:	30'0"
LWL:	22'6"
Beam:	8'7"
Draft:	4'4"
Sail Area:	410 sq.ft.
Mainsail:	230 sq.ft.
Mizzen:	47 sq.ft.
Foresail:	70 sq.ft.
Jib:	63 sq.ft.
Thames meas.:	7 tons
Designer:	Dr. T. Harrison-Butler
Built:	1935 A.H. Moody & Son Ltd.
Price when new:	£500
Owner:	Dr. T. Harrison-Butler

Photo from Joan Jardine-Brown collection.

Vindilis was the first boat to be built by Moody in 1935 to the design of Dr. T Harrison - Butler. The order was placed in the early autumn of 1934. She was an auxiliary Bermudan yawl with a bowsprit and bumpkin. A particularly attractive cruising boat for her time.

Accommodation: From forward, chain locker, foc'sle 2 canvas pipe cots with storage under with cupboards and shelves. Toilet with Baby Blake and wash basin. Saloon with settee berths to port and starboard with padded backs with lockers behind. She had 31 lockers in all. Cabin table folded into floor. Galley being aft on starboard side.

Copy of an original blue print of Vindilis, 1935. Photo from David Moody collection.

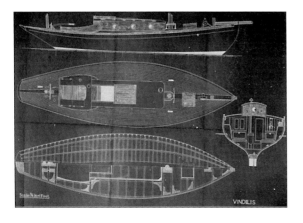

Specification: Keel English oak, stem natural grown English oak. Stern post English oak. Frames English oak. Shelf pitch pine. Bilge and side stringers pitch pine. Deckhouse roof pine tongue and groove covered with canvas. Teak laid decks edge fastened. Deck beams English oak. Main beams English oak. Rudder English oak. Planking is pitch pine apart from the garboard and the first plank being of Scottish elm. Deck work mainly teak. 2 cylinder Stuart Turner petrol engine with reverse gear. Engine mounted aft and under companionway steps. Lead keel. Tiller steering.

Vindilis interior looking forward from companionway steps. You can just see into the forward cabin with one of the pipe cots in the stowed position. Photo from Joan Jardine-Brown collection.

Launching of Zingara by Ellen Harrison-Butler (Dr THB's wife) - quite a precarious occasion in those days, 1936. Photo from Joan Jardine-Brown collection.

Zingara

LOA:	29'6"
LWL:	25'0"
Beam:	8'6"
Draft:	5'0"
Sail area:	460 sq.ft.
Thames meas.:	7 tons

Zingara was the next THB boat to be built by Moody in 1936 and was launched by the designer's wife. Zingara was sold to a Dr. Cargill (a dentist) of Ottawa, Canada. The yacht was transported from the yard to Southampton docks and my father tells the tale of how he travelled in the cockpit as she was transported by road. He would have been around eleven or twelve at the time. She was loaded onto the Steam Ship Montcalm and went to the St. Laurence river. From there she was cruised extensively and sailed on Lake Ontario. Last heard of she was sailing in the U.S.A. She differed from Vindilis as she was a Bermudan cutter. She also had a transom hung rudder. She was powered by a Thorneycroft Handy Billy Petrol engine.

Lindy II

Lindy II was the third THB yacht that came from the Swanwick yard in 1936 built for a Mr Pemberton. She is a sister ship to Vindilis, built on the same moulds. The accommodation did not follow THB design. The bowsprit was longer and

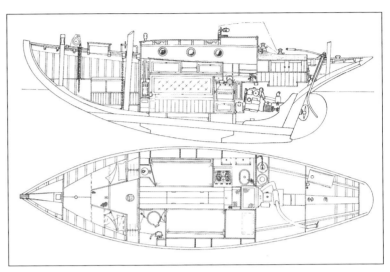

Drawing of Lindy II - sister ship to Vindilis.

the mizzen slightly smaller. Recently we have seen her lying in Eling Creek near Southampton and is being lovingly cared for by her present owner. She is an auxiliary Bermudan yawl powered by a 2 cylinder Stuart Turner petrol engine. Her dimensions are the same as Vindilis.

Edith Rose

LOA:	29'6"
LWL:	23'0"
Beam:	8'6"
Draft:	5'0"
Sail area:	417 sq.ft.
Thames meas.:	7 tons

Edith Rose under construction in the original building shop at Swanwick. Last heard of in Oregon USA. Photo from Joan Jardine-Brown collection.

Edith Rose was the fourth and last of the THB designs to be built by the Company in 1937 for Mr. Crossley. Being designed on the metacentric method, she had the same dimensions as Vindilis except she was six inches longer on the waterline. This yacht was perfectly balanced although some internal ballast had to be added later. She was a Bermudan cutter with a bowsprit and canoe stern.

Photo from Joan Jardine-Brown collection.

Delight

LOA:	32'0"
LWL:	26'0"
Beam:	9'0"
Draft:	5'0"
Sail area:	580 sq.ft.
Thames meas.:	9 tons
Designer:	Frederick Shepherd *MINA* (of 199 Piccadilly, London)
Built:	1935 A.H. Moody & Son Ltd.
Owner:	T.W. Holland, Kent
Cost when new:	£465 (including plans)

Delight was, to use Dr. Harrison-Butler's words, "Vindilis' nursery mate". Both boats were in build together. The yacht was to be completed by Easter 1935.

Accommodation: The after lobby to be fitted up with one starboard berth with drawers under. The portside to contain toilet, fitted with a Blakes Victory W.C. The W.C. compartment to be painted white with usual shelves, coat hooks and fittings. The saloon with 2 settee berths 6'4" long - one port and one starboard with lockers, sideboard and cupboards to be in teak. Aft end of the saloon on starboard, is the galley with stove and cupboards for stowage. A suitable teak table about 3'4" long to be fitted. Forecastle: an oil cooker to be supplied by owner but fitted standing on a lead lined base with protective sheet of lead at back. Cupboard to be fitted on port side also the sail bin as shown with chain locker and seat to port. Foc'sle to be fitted in teak battened sides.

Specification: Keel to be of sound English elm to receive 2.75 tons of lead on keel as ballast. Also half a ton of inside lead ballast in handy pigs to trim yacht to design load. Stem, and stern post to be grown English oak free from all defects. Deadwoods, timbers and beams to be best English oak. Planking to be of selected pitch pine. The covering boards and centre planks to be of teak, the rest to be teak laid in parallel planks. The seams to be caulked in brown oakum and payed with Jefferys Best Marine Glue. All deck work to be in best teak. Build stringers to be pitch pine. Tanks - 60 gallon fresh water tank with a copper fuel tank. The mast is to be Baltic pine and other spars of Norway spruce. Powered by a 4 cylinder Morris paraffin. Bronze tiller.

Eila

LOA:	35'7"
LWL:	26'6"
Beam:	9'0"
Draft:	5'0"
Sail area:	559 sq.ft.
Thames meas.:	9 tons
Designer:	F. Shepherd
Built:	1935
A.H. Moody & Son Ltd.	
Owner:	
	Mr. Stafford Bourne, London

Photo by Beken of Cowes.

Eila was a very early boat to be built by Moody and was built for a very keen and dedicated yachtsman. She was powered by a 4 cylinder Morris petrol engine and would have a similar specification to that of Fubbs. Her frames, stem and stern post and horn timbers would have been in English oak and her keel would have been elm. Her ballast keel would be lead with pitch pine planking. Her deck work would have been teak. Her mast and spars would have been of silver spruce. Note that these early designs also had bowsprits. Note the tapered and sculptured tops to the mast. She had tiller steering and a large cockpit. This yacht using our price formula per ton, would have cost approximately £900 in 1935.

Photo from Mrs Margaret Williamson collection.

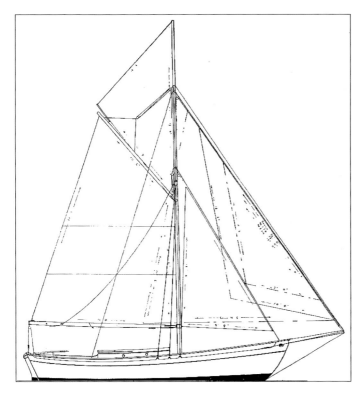

Andrillot

LOA:	25'3"
LWL:	21'0"
Beam:	7'2"
Draft:	4'6"
Sail area:	370 sq.ft.
Thames meas.:	5 tons

Designer:
Laurent Giles & Partners

Built: Spring 1936
A.H. Moody & Son Ltd.

Owner: Mr R. Kinnersley
Guernsey C.I.

Cost when Built: £310

Andrillot was designed by John Laurent Giles in 1936. She was fitted with a gaff rig at the request of the owner. She was not fitted with the Bermudan rig as it had not been completely accepted by the cruising fraternity. To my excitement, following research on this craft from various sources, she was adopted to be the first Vertue, bearing sail number 1.This class has become legendary and Moodys are proud to have played their part at the beginning and she is still in service today.

Accommodation: Deemed to be a little unusual for small boats in this country and found to be more popular in the United States. From forward, chain locker and stowage, fore cabin with two built in berths with stowage under. Saloon with settee berth to starboard with oilskin locker, galley and stowage opposite on portside. As there was no engine, the sails were stowed under the companionway stairs with the water tank being fitted under the cockpit floor.

Specification: The design brief states the yacht is to be 'simply but well constructed in all respects to the satisfaction of the architects.' Keel in English elm, stem, sternpost and deadwood in English oak. Frames to be grown English oak. Frames to be in one piece if available or with lapped butts. Spaced three feet apart, one extra frame in way of mast. Timbers steam bent English oak spaced nine inches. Floors English oak on all grown frames. Wrought iron floors on steamed timbers between each pair of grown frames in way of keel. Planking to be carvel laid of Oregon pine or red pine in good lengths. To be efficiently caulked and stopped, garboard strakes to be English elm. Transom to be mahogany. Stringers and shelf Oregon pine in one length. Deck beams to be red pine apart from in way of mast where English oak. Carlines, hanging lodging knees and Mast Partners to be English oak. Decks to be canvas covered white pine tongue and groove. Deck work to be mainly mahogany. Tiller English oak. Ballast keel to be accurately cast of iron. Mast and spars to be of silver spruce or Oregon pine. Sails to be of best American cotton by Cranfield and Carter.

Photo by Beken of Cowes

Mystery

LOA:	39'0"
LWL:	26'2"
Beam:	8'7"
Draft:	5'5"
Sail area:	598 sq.ft.
Thames meas.:	10 tons
Designed by:	Robert Clark
Built:	1936 A.H. Moody & Son Ltd.
Owner:	F.P. Usborne Southampton

Mystery was the first yacht to be designed by Robert Clark. When launched she was painted a dark colour. It is interesting to see the changes that have occurred in design in the twenty two years between this design and the Pym and Orthops to be seen later. The owner had been the past secretary of the Royal Yachting Association. She proved to be most successful as a cruiser racer.

Accommodation: Fore peak for sail stowage. Foc'sle with two pipe cots, locker and toilet, saloon with 2 x 6'6" berths, table, drawers and lockers. Quarter berth to port, galley to starboard, with chart table over. She had a raised coach roof with skylight and a large self draining cockpit.

Tiller steering and a Gray "Sea scout" engine.

Specification: Oak stem, stern post, horn timbers, oak timbers and bent frames, elm keel, lead ballast keel. Pitch pine planking, pine decks canvas covered. Teak deck work, Spruce mast and spars and was complete with upholstery and sails.

Photo by Beken of Cowes.

Fubbs

LOA:	37' 4"
LWL:	27'6"
Beam:	9'4"
Draft:	5'5"
Sail area:	573 sq.ft.
Thames meas.:	11 tons
Designed by:	F. Shepherd
Built:	1937 A.H. Moody & Son Ltd.
Owner:	V. N. Peel Kensington

Fubbs is a yacht typical of the Shepherd's design of her day. Her cutter rig made her ideal for extensive cruising. She was reputed to have been a first class sea boat with pleasing lines. She was easily identified as she had a large doghouse and deck space, with tiller steering.

Accommodation: Foc'sle with two cot frames with necessary locker and cupboards. Aft of the foc'sle is the toilet to port and hanging space to starboard. The saloon is well appointed with the built-in settee berths. Cupboards, lockers and table. Aft of the saloon to port is the galley and to starboard is the chart space and cupboards. Large doghouse and self draining cockpit. Powered by a four cylinder Parsons 20 HP engine situated under the cockpit floor.

Specification: Includes oak stem stern post and horn timbers. Oak frames and elm keel. Lead ballast keel. Pitch pine planking. Teak decks and deck work. Complete with silver spruce mast, upholstery and sails.

Photo by Beken of Cowes

Silver Streak

LOA:	44'6"
LWL:	31'8"
Beam:	10'2"
Draft:	6'0"
Sail area:	775 sq.ft.
Thames meas.:	15 tons
Designed by:	F. Shepherd
Built:	1937 A.H. Moody & Son Ltd.
Owner:	H.R. Watt Isle of Wight

Silver Streak is an auxiliary ketch and has been extensively cruised in South African waters. Was built to a high specification and is undoubtedly a first class yacht. The photograph gives some idea of the pleasing lines although having rather high freeboard.

Accommodation: Foc'sle with two pipe cots, lockers, cupboards and toilet. Aft of the foc'sle is the galley to port. Cooking stove and sink. To starboard is a second toilet. Saloon with two built-in settee berths, table, cupboards etc. Aft of saloon to starboard is the chart space. Hanging space to port. She has a large cockpit with wheel steering.

Specification: Oak stem, stern post and horn timbers. Oak frames, bent timbers. Teak planking and teak deck work. She is fitted with an Ailsa Craig diesel engine under the cockpit floor. Silver spruce mast and spars. Complete with sails and upholstery.

Photo by Beken of Cowes

Triune of Troy

Channel class

LOA:	37'9"
LWL:	26'0"
Beam:	8'8"
Draft:	6'0"
Sail area:	600 sq.ft.
Thames meas.:	10 tons
Designer:	Laurent Giles & Partners
Built:	1938 A.H. Moody & Son Ltd.
Owner:	Lord Russell of Liverpool, London

Kayak

Channel Class

LOA:	37'8"
LWL:	26'2"
Beam:	8'7"
Draft:	6'0"
Sail area:	750 sq.ft.
Thames meas.:	10 tons
Designer:	Laurent Giles & Partners
Built:	1938 A.H. Moody & Son Ltd.
Owner:	D.D. Capper, Sarisbury Green

Photo by Beken of Cowes

Amokura

LOA:	50'3"
LWL:	37'7"
Beam:	12'0"
Draft:	7'0"
Sail area:	1020 sq.ft.
Thames meas.:	24 tons
Lloyds +100:	A1 class
Designed by:	F. Shepherd
Built:	1939
A.H. Moody & Son Ltd.	
Owner:	
Major E.S. Harston OBE	
Swanwick Shore	

Photo by Beken of Cowes

Amokura was commissioned and used in the latter part of 1939 and then laid up during World War II. She was raced successfully in the immediate post war years with considerable success. She was cruised extensively and was proven as a good sea boat. A sister ship, the Glaramara, was built off the same lines in 1947 for Sir Philip Bowyer-Smyth of Eton Square, London, who had been a Colonial

Officer in West Africa. Both Glaramara and Amokura was built under Lloyds Register of Ships classification. The photograph illustrates the pleasing lines and the power of this excellent yacht.

Accommodation: Foc'sle fitted with one built in berth and one pipe cot. With lockers and cupboards, cruise toilet and chain locker. After foc'sle is the galley with sink, cupboards, plate racks and food cupboard to port. The cooking stove, refrigerator and lockers etc to starboard. The main saloon is spacious with two Pullman berths and on the port side there is a return seat, ample locker space, hanging space, drawers etc. A heating stove is provided on the forward saloon bulkhead. A swinging table is fitted and the saloon is upholstered. Aft of the saloon to port is the owner's toilet and wash space with fitted cupboards. The companionway leads to a lobby between the toilet and wash space. After the lobby is a double cabin with two built-in berths, dressing table, wardrobe, lockers etc. There is a bridge deck and a very nice doghouse and self draining cockpit. Wheel steering. Fuel tank for the diesel engine (Enfield 15bhp) is in the cockpit. The engine is under the bridge deck. She carries 50 gallons of fuel and 140 gallons of water.

Specification: Includes oak stem, stern post and horn timbers and oak frames. Elm keel, lead ballast keel, pitch pine planking. Teak decks and deck work. Pitch pine spars. Yacht complete with sails, rigging and upholstery.

Photo by Beken of Cowes

Josephine II

LOA:	32'0"
LWL:	25'4"
Beam:	7'6"
Draft:	5'0"
Sail area:	323 sq.ft.
Thames meas.:	7 tons
Designed by:	Knud H. Reimers
Built:	1939 A.H. Moody & Son Ltd.
Owner:	Mr Cosby Smallpiece, Swanwick Shore

Josephine II is similar in every respect to Cohoe but in the building of Cohoe the yacht was given more freeboard and length in the water line and more sheer. She is in all ways identical to many of this large Tumlar design and is a very fast cruiser racer yacht. The photograph shows the pleasing lines of Josephine and for her size is an outstanding yacht.

Accommodation: Foredeck for sail stowage, foc'sle with 2 pipe cots, saloon with 2 berths, table, drawers and lockers. The galley is situated aft of the saloon to port and aft again is a large stowage space and chart table. To starboard is fitted a quarter berth. She has a large self draining cockpit with tiller steering and has a raised coach roof from right forward.

Specification: Includes oak main centreline framing with oak timbers, lead keel, mahogany planking and western red cedar decks, canvas covered. Mahogany deck work. She has a Stuart Turner 4 bhp petrol engine. Silver spruce mast and spars. Her inventory includes sails and upholstery.

Josephine II

These two photographs capture Josephine II under construction in the building shop. The top picture shows her keel and centreline in place with the moulds ready to be planked. The lower picture shows her now fully planked in mahogany.

These photographs were kindly provided by Mrs Elizabeth Jowett, daughter of Mr Cosby Smallpiece who was the owner of the Josephine yachts.

Craft Built for the Admiralty

1939-1945

This section illustrates the craft built by Moody for the Admiralty during hostilities. It gives the build numbers, their service history and their subsequent disposal details.

25ft Fast Motor Boat (FMB)

Photo from the Small Craft Group.

LOA: 25'0" ● *Beam:* 7'0" ● *Draft:* 1'8" ● *Weight:* 1.9 tons ● *Engine:* Ferry Ford V8 Petrol ● *Speed:* 16-18 knots ● *Admiralty numbers:* 39507 - 39512 (Contract CP61254/39) and 40168 - 40171 (Contract CP8E/74814/40) ● 10 built

Disposal
25ft FMB

39507	S	Delivered to GEO Wilson, Sunbury 7/47
39508	L	WOC 1952 no trace. Lost with HERO or at Aden??
39509	S	Handed over to Hocking Brothers, Plymouth 4/48
39510	L	Presumed lost with PELICAN 7/42
39511	S	Handed over to Hocking Brothers, Plymouth 6/47 (s)
39512	S	Disposed of or BU at Freetown 9/47 (s)
40168	T	Presumed transferred with SUTLEJ to India 7/47
40169	T	Presumed transferred with SUTLEJ to India 7/47
40170	T	Presumed transferred with SUTLEJ to India 7/47
40171	T	Presumed transferred with JUMNA to India 7/47

25ft Motor Surveying Boat (MSB)

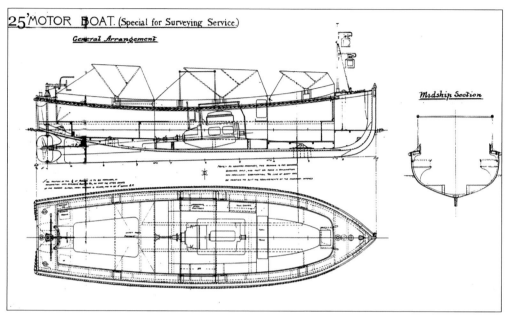

Photo from the Small Craft Group.

LOA: 25'0" ● *Beam:* 7'3" ● *Draft:* 2'2" ● *Weight:* 3.3 tons ● *Speed:* 7 knots
● *Admiralty numbers:* 41568 - 41569 *Engine:* Ferry BM4 petrol (Contract CP
8E/60580/41) 41777 - 41778 *Engine:* Ferry BM4 petrol (Contract CP97264/41) 42354
- 42356 *Engine:* Parsons H4M petrol (Contract CP22764/42) ● 7 built

Disposal
25ft MSB

41568	T	Sold with PROTEA to South Africa 10/47
41569	T	Sold with PROTEA to South Africa 10/47
41777	S	HO to F. Watts Gosport 3/48 deleted 6/48
41778	S	HO to Allan and Sons, Gillingham for C and M 3/48
42354	S	Sold to Mr. L.W.J. Doine, Shoreburyness 10/70
42355	S	HO to Allan and Sons, Gillingham for C and M 3/48
42356	R	Assumed returned with JAN VAN BRAKEL 1949

28ft Motor Survey Boat (MSB)

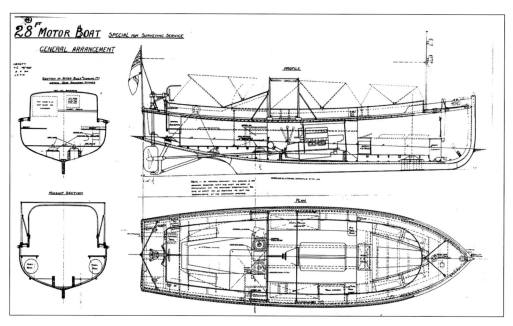

Photo from the Small Craft Group.

LOA: 28'0" ● *Beam:* 7'11" ● *Draft:* 2'6" ● *Weight:* 5.1 tons ● *Speed:* 7 knots
● *Admiralty numbers:* 37290 to 37291 *Engine:* Ferry BM petrol (Contract
CP39180/37) 4187 to 4189 *Engine:* Parsons H4M petrol (Contract CP 18159/41)
41775 to 41776 *Engine:* Parsons H4M petrol (Contract CP97264/41) 42357 to 42358
Engine: Parsons H4M petrol (Contract CP 22764/42) ● 9 built

Disposal
28ft MSB

37290	L	Lost to Japanese forces at Singapore?
37290	L	Lost to Japanese forces at Singapore?
41775	S	Disposed of at Rosyth 6/78
41776	S	Sold to Belsize Southampton 12/61
4187	*	Last known at Singapore 11/62
4188	S	Sold to Belsize Southampton 11/61
4189	*	Last known at Portsmouth 1962
42357	S	Sold at Sheerness 9/58
42358	S	To be sold with SHACKLETON 2/63

32ft Motor Cutter (MC)

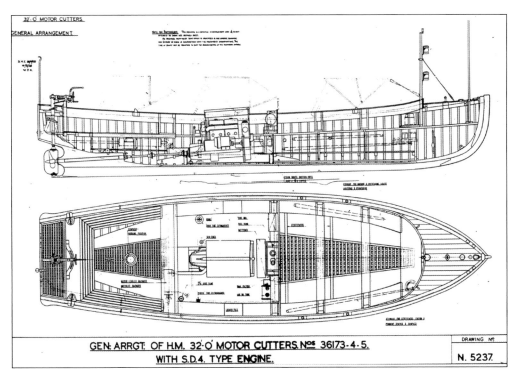

GEN: ARRGT: OF H.M. 32·0' MOTOR CUTTERS. Nos 36173-4-5. WITH S.D.4. TYPE ENGINE.

DRAWING Nº N. 5237

Photo from the Small Craft Group.

LOA: 32'0" • *Beam:* 8'7" • *Draft:* 1'7" • *Weight:* 3.5 tons • *Engine:* Dorman 4DSM diesel • *Speed:* 7.5 knots • *Admiralty numbers:* 43705 to 43716 (Contract CP92181/43) 44902 to 44913 (Contract CP83070/44) 45869 to 45874 (Contract CP67724/45 cancelled 9/45) • 24 built

Disposal

32ft MC

43705	S	Sold to Mr. T. Balance, Burntisland 11/56	43706	S	Sold to Mr. A.V. Jackson, Peterborough 11/57
43707	L	Lost overboard from THESEUS in a gale 3/49	43708	S	Sold to Mr. A.V. Jackson, Peterborough 12/61
43709	B	BTP at Rosyth 8/57	43710	S	Sold to Drake Metal Salvage, Plymouth 8/56
43711	B	BTP at Rosyth 6/57	43712	T	Sold with VENERABLE to the Dutch 5/48
43713	S	Sold at Hong Kong 1/47	43714	S	Sold at Malta 7/65
43715	S	Disposed of at Gibraltar 1/58	43716	S	For disposal at Chatham 1946
44902	*	last known at BEAULY FIRTH 5/45 deleted 1948	44903	S	For sale at Chatham 8/73
44904	*	Last known at BRNC Dartmouth 1960	44905	*	Last known at BRNC Dartmouth 1960
44906	S	Sold to Belsize, Southampton 12/61	44907	S	Sold to Mr. A.V. Jackson, Peterborough 9/68
44908	T	Sold with COLOSSUS to the French 1951	44909	*	For disposal 1962 details not sure
44910 to 44913	S	Sold to Belsize, Southampton 10/52			

36ft Harbour Launch (HL)

LOA: 36ft 0" • *Beam:* 9'9"
• *Draft:* 1'8" • *Weight:* 6 tons
• *Speed:* 8 knots
• *Admiralty numbers:* 42619
to 42624 Calvin F4 petrol
(Contract CP 50306/42)
42821 to 42826 Vosper V8 Ford
petrol (Contract CP68168/42)
43607 to 43614 Vosper V8 Ford
petrol (Contract CP84577/434)
44276 to 44281 Berguis F4
petrol (Contract CP74448/44)
442760 to 441673 Vosper V8
petrol (Contract CP100972/44)
45991 to 45994 Vosper V8
petrol (Contract CP76550/45)
• 32 built

Photo from the Small Craft Group.

Disposal
36ft HL

42619	S	HO to Emsworth Shipyard for C&M 7/46	42620	*	last known with Maidstone SCC 7/60
42621	L	Lost at sea whilst in transit 10/45	42622	S	HO to Woodnutts Bembridge for C&M 1/46
42623	S	HO to Lymington slipway for C&M 8/46	42624	S	HO to Lymington slipway for C&M 8/46
42821	P	Became pulling boat 508/47 Malta 1947	42822	B	BTP at Malta 1949
42823	B	Scrapped at Trincomalee 3/46	42824	S	Condemned and sold at Trincomalee 2/49
42825	S	HO to Itchener shipyard for C&M 2/47	42826	*	last known with British Overseas Airways 1943
43607	W	WOC 1949 last known with F.O. Holland 1945	43608	S	HO to F. Watts, Gosport for C&M 5/51
43609	T	Transferred to War dept 12/47	43610	L	Total loss at Singapore 1948
43611	S	Sold to Mr. J.T. Granger, Dover 3/59	43612	S	Sold to Timbacraft Ltd. Rhu 8/57
43613	W	WOC 1952	43614	L	Lost due to damage 1965
441670	S	For disposal at Singapore 12/53	441671	W	Presumed stolen 5/47 at Singapore WOC 1947
441672	T	Transferred to War dept 12/47	441673	S	For disposal by BSDM at Port Said 7/50
44276	T	Transferred to War dept 12/47	44277	S	Disposed off locally at Singapore 1948
44278	S	Sold at Hong Kong 12/50	44279	S	Sold at Sydney 1948
44280	S	For disposal at Bombay 5/46	44281	S	For disposal at Bombay 5/46
45911	S	Sold to Belsize, Southampton 5/72	45992	B	BTP at Devonport 6/62
45993 & 45994 cancelled 9/45					

36ft Motor Pulling Pinnace (MPP)

Photo from the Small Craft Group.

LOA: 36'0" ● *Beam:* 9'9" ● *Draft:* 1'8" ● *Weight:* 6 tons ● *Engine:* Dorman 4DSM diesel ● *Speed:* 7.5 knots ● 6 built ● *Admiralty numbers:* 41601 to 41606 (Contract CP8E/60584/41)

Disposal
36ft MPP

41601	*	last known with Peterhead SCC 4/63
41602	B	BTP at Portsmouth 1957
41603	S	For sale at RNAY Sydenham, Belfast 6/73
41604	S	Sold to Belsize Southampton 1/63
41605	S	Sold to Belsize Southampton 8/57
41606	B	Burnt at Singapore 2/62

42ft Naval Storing Tender (NST)

Photo from the Small Craft Group.

LOA: 39'5" ● *Beam:* 12'6" ● *Draft:* 2'4" ● *Weight:* 19.2 tons ● *Engine:* 2x Perkins P4M diesels ● *Speed:* 7.92 knots ● *Admiralty numbers:* 54189 to 54192 ● 4 built

Disposal
42ft NST

54189	unknown	
54190	unknown	
54191	FS	6/83 DE Sold 7/83
54192	FD	4/77 Hong Kong area

45ft Fast Motor Boat and Barge (FMB)

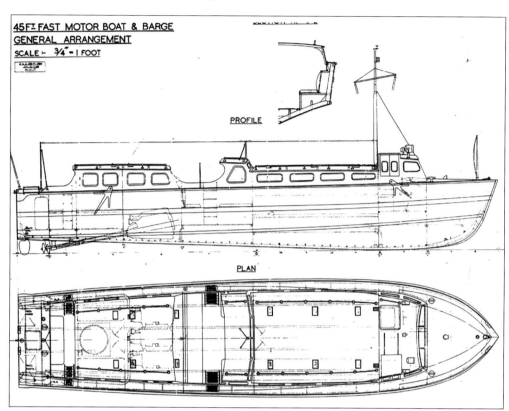

Photo from the Small Craft Group.

LOA: 45'0" ● *Beam:* 10'6" ● *Draft:* 2'0" ● *Weight:* 8 tons ● *Engines:* 3x Vosper Mark 3 Ford V8 petrol ● *Speed:* 18 knots ● *Admiralty numbers:* 40210 to 40212 (Contract CP8E/91482/40) ● 3 built

Disposal
45ft FMB

40210	S	HO to Erskins of Belfast for C&M 4/46
40211	S	HO to Marine Craft Boat Builders 4/46
40212	S	HO to Timba Craft Rhu for C&M 7/46

Landing Craft Assault (LCA)

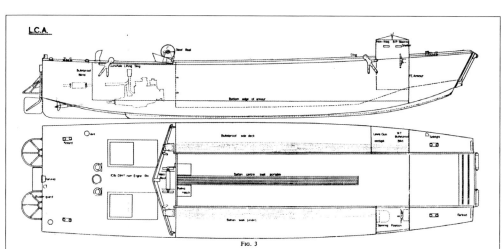

Photo from the Philip Simons Collection.

LOA: 41'6" ● *Beam:* 10'0" ● *Draft:* 2'3" ● *Weight:* 9/13tons displacement ● *Engines:* 2x Ford V8 petrol ● *Speed:* 10 knots ● All Landing Craft Assault craft were subcontracted from Thorneycroft ● 10 built

LCA No:	Completed	Disposal
LCA23	July 1923	Cannibalised, fittings removed and hulls transferred to RAF as target 3/44
LCA24	July 1940	U/S. Engines etc removed. Scrapped Rosneath 5/44
LCA33	August 1940	Lost in East Indies date unknown 6/44
LCA34	August 1940	Engines etc removed WOC 3/44
LCA35	October 1940	Lost operation TORCH November 1942
LCA36	October 1940	Lost in Gareloch in use as Gash Barge 12/46 WOC 1/47
LCA78	November 1940	Beached whilst on tow from Algiers to Djidjelli WOC 1/47
LCA79	November 1940	Lost in Middle East 1941
LCA80	November 1940	Lost in Middle East 1941
LCA81	December 1940	Lost in Middle East 1941

Harbour Defence Motor Launch (HDML)
ML1221, built by A.H. Moody & Son Ltd.

Photo from the Imperial War Museum.

LOA: 72'0" ● *LWL:* 69'0" ● *Beam:* 15'0" ● *Draft:* 4.5'/5.5' ● *Displacement:* 54 tons (deep load) ● 2x 300 bhp Gardner diesels ● *Speed:* 11.4 knots continuous cruising and 12.5 knots max. ● *Range:* 1000 miles at 12 knots. 2000 miles at 10 knots ● Crew 2 officers, 2 Petty officers, 8-10 ratings. Armaments - many variations by 1945 ● Most had 2 x 20mm, 4x.303 Vickers in 2 twins plus 4-8 depth charges ● Construction round bilge double diagonal mahogany (a few were larch planked) ● 16 built at Swanwick.

Disposal

HDML		HDML	
1067	FDB 34. Sold to France 1/48 as VP24	1068	FDB 54 Sold to China 1947
1148	Royal Indian Navy 1943. Sold 1947	1149	Greek Kissoura 9/45. FD 1962
1221	Greek Bizani on loan 8/45. FD 1962	1222	Sold 1946
1276	FDB 63 sold 7/47	1277	To Israel 1946
1278	FD 1946 sold as Yacht Lady Walrus	1374	To Burma Government 4/64
1375	Greek Kastraki on loan 11/45 FD 1961	1421	FDB 77. Sold 1947
1422	ASL 15 FD 846 Yacht Violanda. FPV	1432	To France 1946 as VP 747
	Thomas S. Richardson 1951. Yacht TSR	1488	Lent to Burma 8/45 Gifted to Burma 1/48
1489	FDB 38 to Royal Netherlands Navy 1945		

Timber Yachts

1946-1970

*This section illustrates a selection
of timber yachts built by Moody.*

Cohoe

LOA:	32'0"
LWL:	25'6"
Beam:	7'5"
Draft:	5'0
Sail area:	340 sq.ft.
Thames meas.:	7 tons
Designed by:	
	Knud H. Reimers
Built:	1946
A.H. Moody & Son Ltd.	
Owner: K. Adlard Coles	
	Bursledon

Photo by Beken of Cowes

The 7 ton auxiliary sloop, 'Cohoe' built for the well known yachtsman, K. Adlard Coles, needs little introduction as everyone will recall her winning the 1950 Transatlantic race. It was the subject of his book 'North Atlantic'. This book explains in great detail how well this little yacht stood up to the worst hazards the Atlantic could offer. A.H. Moody & Son are proud to have built this famous yacht. Cohoe was built to a high class specification. The photograph shows Cohoe in more pleasant conditions but this yacht has seen many storms and has won many races under the most difficult conditions.

Accommodation: Fore peak. Foc'sle with 2 pipe cots and lockers. After foc'sle to port is the toilet. To starboard is ample hanging space. Next is saloon with 2 settee berths and folding table. Lockers and cupboards. Aft of saloon to port is the galley with cooking stove, sink and cupboards etc. To starboard is a quarter berth with chart table over. She has a large self draining cockpit and a very nice doghouse. Tiller steering.

Specification: Main centreline structure in oak with oak timbers. Mahogany planking western red cedar decks canvas covered. Mahogany deck work, lead keel. A water motor. 8bhp petrol engine with folding propeller, silver spruce spars complete with sails and upholstery.

Photo by Beken of Cowes

Drolene II

Brittany Class

LOA:	31'4"
LWL:	25'0"
Beam:	8'3"
Draft:	5'3"
Sail area:	475 sq.ft.
Thames meas.:	8 tons
Designed by: Laurent Giles & Partners	
Built: 1948 A.H. Moody & Son Ltd.	
Owner:	W.G. Gill Surrey

Drolene has been highly successful in both racing and cruising. She was cruised extensively each season since she was built and remained in the same ownership. The photograph shows Drolene II to be both a pretty and useful type of boat typical of the designers.

Accommodation: Foc'sle fitted with pipe cot, racks stowage space and toilet. Aft of foc'sle to port an oil skin and sea boot locker. To starboard a wardrobe. The saloon is well appointed with two settee berths, folding table and ample cupboard and locker space. Aft of saloon to port is the galley with cooking stove and sink. Ample locker space and to starboard is a quarter berth with chart table and locker space. A self draining cockpit is provided with ample locker space. Tiller steering, pleasing and useful doghouse. She has a 8 BHP Stuart Turner petrol engine installed and has electric light throughout. Water capacity is 25 gallons, fuel capacity is 8 gallons.

Specification: Oak stem, stern post, horn timbers and stern knees. Grown oak frames with 2 oak bent timbers between. Elm keel and false keel. Lead ballast keel. Mahogany planking, mahogany deck work, silver spruce mast and spars, canvas covered western red cedar decks, fully equipped with sails upholstery etc.

Photo by Beken of Cowes

Pocahontas

LOA:	31'1"
LWL:	24'0"
Beam:	7'5"
Draft:	5'9"
Sail area:	465 sq.ft.
Thames meas.:	7 tons
Designed by:	
Laurent Giles & Partners	
Built:	1948
A.H. Moody & Son Ltd.	
Owner:	
Mr. R. Plunkett-Green	
East Sussex	

Pocahontas was one of the original Royal Naval Sailing Association designs to be built. She has had a most successful racing and cruising record and is a fine example of this very popular design. The photograph shows Pocahontas to be a steady craft with pleasing lines.

Accommodation: From forward: Fore peak for sail storage, foc'lse with pipe cot and hanging cupboard to port. Racked sail bin to starboard and hanging locker. The toilet is situated right forward in the foc'sle. The main saloon is fitted with a settee berths port and starboard and ample locker and storage space. Aft of the saloon to port is the galley with lockers and cupboards etc. and to starboard is a quarter berth with chart table over. She has a large self draining cockpit. Tiller steering. She is fitted with a 4 BHP Stuart Turner Petrol engine. There is no doghouse, but a raised coach roof right forward.

Specification: Includes oak stem, stern post and stem and stern knees. Elm keel. Iron ballast keel. Oak timbers and silver spruce longitudinals. West red cedar canvas covered decks, mahogany deck work and silver spruce mast and spars. Complete with sails and upholstery.

Photo from David Moody collection.

Fandango

LOA:	43'2"
LWL:	33'0
Beam:	9'1"
Draft:	7'2"
Sail area:	643 sq.ft.
Thames meas.:	12 tons
Designed by: Laurent Giles & Partners	
Built: 1949 A.H. Moody & Son Ltd.	
Owner: Major G. Potter E.W., M.C. Churston Ferrers, S. Devon	

Photo by Beken of Cowes

Built for serious off-shore racing. She has had a very successful career and has won many major prizes. She was one of the fastest boats of her time in Great Britain.

Accommodation: From forward, sail stowage in fore peak, double berth fore cabin with toilet. Saloon with 2 settee berths, lockers and cupboards and table. Aft of saloon is a chart table to starboard. Oilskin locker and galley to port. There is a quarter berth to starboard. She will comfortably sleep six people.

Specification: Fandango was built to a high class specification with oak stem, elm keel, web frames, longitudinal stringers, plywood bulkheads and double skin and western red cedar planking. Western red cedar deck work. Her decks are double skin, the lower skin being western red cedar and the top skin teak. She is fitted with a 8 BHP Stuart Turner petrol engine. She has wheel steering. A large self draining cockpit and adequate locker space. Sheet and halyard winches as necessary. Fandango has a very pleasant deckline.

Photo from David Moody collection.

Photo by Beken of Cowes

Anna

LOA:	22'6"
LWL:	17'0"
Beam:	6'6"
Draft:	4'0"
Sail area:	208 sq.ft.
Thames meas.:	4 tons
Designed by:	
	W.L. Hobbs
Built:	1952
A.H. Moody & Son Ltd.	
Owner: Edward J. Freer,	
	Leicester

The auxilary sloop, Anna, was intended to be a day cruising boat for the occasional weekend away. She has been raced on occasions and proved quite fast. I looked at Anna everyday during my younger life as she was moored on a swinging mooring outside Myrtle Cottage.

Accommodation: She was a well built little boat and quite roomy for her size. Her foc'sle accommodates a pipe cot and toilet whilst her saloon has 2 settee berths, a cooking stove and wash basin.

Specification: Her mast is stepped on deck in a tabernacle. A large self draining cockpit with tiller steering. First class materials were used in her construction. She has oak framing and Lagos mahogany planking with all deck work in teak. Fitted with a 4 BHP single cylinder Stuart Turner petrol engine. She comes with a suit of sails and upholstery.

Photo by Beken of Cowes

Josephine IV

LOA:	39'0"
LWL:	27'8"
Beam:	8'7"
Draft:	6'4"
Sail area:	570 sq.ft.
Thames meas.:	10 tons
Lloyds +100:	A1 class
Designed by:	James Mc. Gruer
Built:	1953
	A.H. Moody & Son Ltd.
Owner:	Mr. Cosby Smallpiece
	Swanwick Shore

The Josephine is an 8 metre cruiser racer. She been most successful every season since her launching. In addition to being fast she is also comfortable for cruising with very pleasing lines.

Accommodation: From forward: Foc'sle with pipe cot and toilet to port. Sink and cooking stove to starboard. Main saloon is fitted with 2 berths with ample locker space. Aft to port there is a toilet.

Specification: Josephine IV was built under Lloyds supervision and is classed +100 A1. She is to the International 8 metre cruiser racer classification. Includes English oak keel, lead ballast keel, mahogany stem stern post. Stem and stern knee and deadwoods. English oak bent timbers. Lagos mahogany planking. Western red cedar deck, canvas covered. Western red cedar coach roof. Mahogany deck work and doghouse. Silver spruce hollow mast and stainless steel rigging. Complete with sheet and halyard winches. Fresh water capacity 20 gallons. Whilst no engine is fitted, this can be done and the yacht can still remain in the 8 metre cruiser racer class.

Photo by Beken of Cowes

Norlethe

LOA:	42'9"
LWL:	32'6"
Beam:	10'1"
Draft:	7'2"
Sail area:	675 sq.ft.
Thames meas.:	15 tons
Lloyds +100:	A1 class
Designed by:	Frederick R. Parker *MINA*
Built:	1954 A.H. Moody & Son Ltd.
Owner:	Mr. R.R. Burton, Warsash

Norlethe is probably the most outstanding and beautifully designed and built yacht in Britain since the War. She was built for a well-known local yachtsman and has raced most successfully in all conditions and is the holder of many trophies.

Accommodation: From forward: Stowage with chain locker under. Crew's toilet, built in bunk to port, sail stowage and oilskin locker to starboard, after foc'sle. To port, toilet and washing space. To starboard wardrobe and cupboards. Main saloon with two settee berths, lockers, cupboards and folding table. After saloon to port is the galley with cooking stove and quarter berth. To starboard is a sink unit and quarter berth. A well designed doghouse is provided. Engine beneath floor at entrance to yacht. Spacious self draining cockpit with lockers etc. Separate helmsman cockpit with wheel steering, compass fitted to top of steering pedestal. The yacht is finished internally in oak and is complete with upholstery.

Specification: The yacht is built under Lloyds supervision and classed +100 A1. Built to the highest possible specification. She is fitted with a Parsons Prawn 12/24 HP petrol engine and with a Newall Petticrow folding propeller. She is fitted with a large generator and is wired throughout with electric lighting and navigation lights. Norlethe is built of teak planking on oak frames and backbone. Teak laid deck and teak deck work. She has a hollow silver spruce mast, all deck fittings are chromium plated.

Marguerita Helena

Lion Class

LOA:	35'0"
LWL:	24'0"
Beam:	8'9"
Draft:	5'6"
Sail area:	480 sq.ft.
Thames meas.:	9 tons
Lloyds +100:	A1 class
Designed by:	Arthur C. Robb
Built:	1956
A.H. Moody & Son Ltd.	
Owner:	M.H. Godden, Cheltenham

Photo by Beken of Cowes

The Marguerita Helena was shown at the first National Boat Show under the name 'Lioness'. She was one of six yachts built of the Lion Class built by A.H. Moody & Son. Ann Speed (1951) and Sabeema (1954) were both owned by the John Lewis Partnership. Zaida (1952) was owned by Colin Ratsey who was at the time running the American office of Ratsey and Lapthorne sail loft. Half Pint (1953) was owned by J.F. Dibben and Leonita (1955) was owned by F.M. Brown.

Accommodation: From forward, fore peak for sail stowage. Foc'sle with 2 built in berths with locker space under, wardrobe etc. After foc'sle to port galley with cooking stove. To starboard toilet with wash basin. Main saloon with 2 settee berths, table and ample locker and cupboard space. Aft of saloon is an oilskin alcove, lockers etc and to starboard, quarter berth with chart table over. Pleasant doghouse, large self draining cockpit and tiller steering. Engine is situated under entrance to yacht.

Specification: Marguerita Helena was built under Lloyds supervision and classed +100 A1 at Lloyds. She is fitted with a 2 cylinder Stuart Turner 8 BHP petrol engine. She has electric starting and lighting throughout. She is built to a very high class specification including teak laid decks and deck work, Lagos mahogany planking, lead keel, English oak stem sternpost keel and timbers. She has a hollow silver spruce mast, sheet and halyard winches, anchor windlass and all necessary deck fittings.The yachts comes with sails, stainless steel rigging, water capacity 35 gallons and fuel capacity 15 gallons. Similar yachts were exported to the USA and Canada.

Photo by Beken of Cowes

Moonspray

LOA:	40'0"
LWL:	30'0"
Beam:	9'9"
Draft:	6'3"
Sail area:	578 sq.ft.
Thames meas.:	12 tons
Lloyds +100:	A1 class
Designed by:	Frederick R. Parker
	MINA
Built:	1956
A.H. Moody & Son Ltd.	
Owner:	Royal Bath Hotel
	Bournemouth Ltd

Moonspray is one of three yachts built of the same design. Nyala of St. Vincent (owned by C. de Barnard of Orange Hill, St. Vincent) and Sardonyx (owned by Mr Harold F. Edwards of St Albans) are the other two. All these yachts have proved very fast and have won many prizes. They are also very comfortable cruisers. One of these yachts, Nyala of St.Vincent, is owned and cruised in the West Indies.

Accommodation: From forward, large storage space, foc'sle with 2 built in bunks with drawers under, locker space and toilet for crew. To port is situated the owner's toilet and wash basin and on starboard a hanging space and oilskin locker. The saloon has 2 settee berths with drawers under, locker and cupboard space and folding table. After saloon to port is the galley with cooking stove and quarter berth. To starboard is a sink and quarter berth. There is accommodation to sleep 6 people and is finished below in light oak. She has a teak doghouse and engine is situated under entrance to yacht. She has a large self draining cockpit with ample locker space. Wheel steering in a helmsman's cockpit is provided. The compass is mounted on the steering pedestal.

Specification: Moonspray was built under Lloyd's supervision and classed at + 100 A1. She is fitted with a Parson's Prawn 12/24 HP petrol engine with Newall Petticrow stern gear, electric starting and lighting throughout including navigation lights. She is built to a high specification with teak laid decks and teak deck work, splined finished Lagos mahogany planking. Her main framing is mahogany with English Oak bent timbers. Sheet and halyard winches. Anchor windlass and hollow silver spruce mast and spars. Sails by Ratsey and Lapthorne.

Sally Forth

LOA:	37'6"
LWL:	27'6"
Beam:	10'10"
Draft:	4'0" ex plate
Sail area:	600 sq.ft.
Thames meas.:	14 tons
Lloyds +100:	A1 class
Designer:	Frederick R. Parker *MINA*
Built:	1957 A.H. Moody & Son Ltd.
Owner:	J. Stanley Beard *JP FRIBA* Bournemouth

Photo from David Moody collection.

Sally Forth was shown at the 1957/58 National Boat Show. She has proved to be very comfortable cruising yacht and is very fast. She has a centre board and her broad beam gives her very good accommodation.

Accommodation: Her layout is rather unusual and was designed to suit the owner's requirements but of course this could be altered to suit other people. She has a fore peak then a double berth, then a double berth foc'sle with built in bunks lockers and cupboards. Aft of foc'sle is crew's toilet and wash basin etc. to starboard. Owner's toilet and washbasin to port. After this is the spacious saloon with 2 settee berths which can be converted to 4 berths when required. The saloon table and the usual lockers and cupboards. Aft of the saloon is the spacious galley to port and chart table to starboard. The centre board casing is in this area and she has a well proportioned doghouse and large self draining cockpit. Wheel steering with compass mounted on top of the steering pedestal. The mast is stepped on deck in a tabernacle.

Specification: Mahogany keel, stem, sternpost, horn timbers and rudder. Lead ballast keel. Bronze centre plate, Lagos mahogany planking. English oak timbers. Silver spruce shelf and stringers. English oak clamp. Teak laid decks and deck work. Ratsey and Lapthorne sails. Parsons Prawn engine 10/24 BHP. Petrol tank 25 gallons. Water tank 55 gallons. Internally finished in light oak. Blakes toilets.

Photo by Beken of Cowes

Marguerita Helena

LOA:	47'0"
LWL:	34'6"
Beam:	11'4"
Draft:	7'0"
Sail area:	900 sq.ft.
Thames Meas.:	20 tons
Lloyds +100:	A1 class
Designed by:	Frederick R. Parker
	MINA
Built:	1957
A.H. Moody & Son Ltd.	
Owner:	Mrs M.H. Godden
	Cheltenham

Marguerita Helena has been cruised extensively since she was built, but when raced gives a good account for herself.

Accommodation: From forward, the foc'sle has one built in berth and one pipe cot with lockers and cupboards, chain lockers etc. Stowage is right forward. Toilet to port. Galley with stove and sink to starboard. The saloon with 2 settee berths with lockers under, cupboard space and folding table. Owner's toilet to port with shower and wash basin. Aft is the owner's cabin. To starboard is an oilskin locker and aft of this is a quarter berth with chart table over. She has a well designed doghouse, the engine is situated under the entrance to the yacht. A large self draining cockpit with wheel steering and helmsman's seat. The compass is mounted on the pedestal. There is ample locker space in the cockpit. Fuel capacity is 20 gallons. The finish below is light oak. Comfortably sleeps 6 people.

Specification: Built under Lloyds supervision and classed +100 A1. Built to a high specification, fitted with a Parsons Prawn 12/24 HP petrol engine with 2 - 1 reduction gear. Newall Petticrow folding propeller. Electric starting and lighting throughout. Navigation lights. This yacht has teak laid decks and teak deck house. Lagos mahogany planking topside. Splined finish. Mahogany stem, stern post, keel etc. Oak timbers. Hollow silver spruce mast and spars. Anchor windlass and sheet and halyard winches. Sails by Ratsey and Lapthorne.

Pym

LOA:	37'4"
LWL:	27'0"
Beam:	9'0"
Draft:	6'3"
Sail area:	600 sq.ft.
Thames meas.:	12 tons
Lloyds +100:	A1 class
Designer:	Robert Clark
Built:	1958
A.H. Moody & Son Ltd.	
Owner:	
	D.J. Bowyer *DFC*
	Gerrards Cross

Photo by Beken of Cowes

The 9 ton auxiliary sloop, Pym has proved to be the most outstanding boat of her size. During her first season she won many offshore events including the Class III Championship and cruised some 3120 miles. She was also overall winner of the Harwich - Hook race within ten days of her launching. The photograph shows Pym to be a most attractive yacht, well laid out for cruiser racing.

Accommodation: Double sleeping berths in foc'sle. Toilet to port. Large hanging locker and store to starboard. Saloon with settees to port and starboard. Extra pilot berths fitted, port and starboard above settees. Chart table port side aft saloon, galley to starboard. Dog house and self draining cockpit. Tiller steering. Locker space for sails on port and starboard side of cockpit.

Photo from David Moody collection.

Specification: Mahogany keel, stem, stern post, and horn timbers and rudder. Lead ballast keel, Canadian rock elm timbers, galvanized iron floors, spruce bilge stringers and beam shelf, Lagos mahogany planking. Canvas covered plywood decks. Silver spruce mast and spars. Sails by Ratsey and Lapthorne. Powered by a Coventry Victor 14/16 BHP petrol engine with feathering propeller.

Photo by Beken of Cowes

Brynhilde

LOA:	32'6"
LWL:	24'0"
Beam:	8'0"
Draft:	5'8"
Sail area:	430 sq.ft.
Thames Meas.:	7 tons
Lloyds +100:	A1 class
Designer:	Frederick R. Parker
Built:	1958 A.H. Moody & Son Ltd.
Owner:	H. Dick Broom *M.B.E* High Wycombe

•The yacht was intended for both offshore racing and cruising and during the 1958 season has proved quite fast although she was not raced on many occasions.

Accommodation: From forward, storage locker right forward, foc'sle with two built-in berths with lockers under and two cupboards on forward end of berths. Chain locker under foc'sle floor. Toilet to port, hanging locker and shelf to starboard over 25 gallon water tank. Main saloon with two settee berths. Lockers, cupboards and folding table. Galley to port with cooking stove, sink and draining board, lockers and cupboards. Chart table to starboard. Quarter berth on starboard side. Well designed doghouse with engine under floor. Self draining cockpit with wheel steering. Accommodation for five people in comfort. Complete with upholstery and mahogany interior finish.

Specification: Brynhilde was built under Lloyds supervision and was classed +100A1. Fitted with an 8BHP Stuart Turner petrol engine turning a two bladed propeller and a large type dynamo. She is fitted with electric lighting throughout including navigation lights. She is fitted with teak laid decks and teak deck work. Lagos mahogany planking and the topside spleens are splined finished. She has a hollow silver spruce mast and spars and terylene sails by Ratsey and Lapthorne.

Orthops

LOA:	36'0"
LWL:	26'0"
Beam:	9'6"
Draft:	4'11"
Sail area:	546 sq.ft.
Thames meas.:	11 tons
Lloyds +100:	A1 class
Designer:	Robert Clark
Built:	1958
A.H. Moody & Son Ltd.	
Owner:	Mr Hugh Orr
	Beckenham

Photo by Beken of Cowes

Photo from David Moody collection.

Orthops was on show at the National London Boat Show in January 1959.

Accommodation: Her layout from forward is a chain locker, a 2 berth sleeping cabin, toilet and wash basin to port, well equipped galley to starboard. A spacious main saloon, fitted with full length sleeping berths. Aft on port side is the chart table with drawers etc. A hinged bucket seat with oilskin locker aft of saloon to starboard. A pleasing and useful doghouse. Large self draining cockpit with tiller steering. She will sleep 4 people in comfort and comes complete with upholstery. Interior finish is in Honduras cedar.

Specification: Built under Lloyds supervision and classed +100A1. She is fitted with a 14/16 BHP Coventry Victor petrol engine with electric starting and electric lighting throughout including navigation lights. She has teak laid decks and teak deck work. Lagos mahogany topside planking and teak planking below the waterline. Hollow silver spruce mast and spars and has Terylene sails. The yacht is intended for serious off shore racing and family cruising. During her first season proved very fast.

Photo by Beken of Cowes

Contango

Jolina class

LOA:	35'0"
LWL:	25'0"
Beam:	8'9"
Draft:	5'8"
Sail area:	603 sq.ft.
Thames meas.:	9 tons
Designer:	C.A. Nicholson
Built:	1959
	A.H. Moody & Son Ltd.
Owner:	Dr. I. Kinross
	Fareham

Toretta

LOA:	36'8"
LWL:	26'0"
Beam:	9'6"
Draft:	4'9"
Sail area:	546 sq.ft.
Thames meas.:	11 tons
Lloyds +100:	A1 class
Designer:	Robert Clark Ltd
Built:	1959
	A.H. Moody & Son Ltd.
Owner:	P.J. Agg
	Surrey

Photo by Beken of Cowes

Photo by Beken of Cowes

Mia

Mia class

LOA:	43'0"
LWL:	33'3"
Beam:	10'10"
Draft:	6'0"
Sail area:	693 sq.ft.
Thames meas.:	17 tons
Lloyds +100:	A1 class
Designer:	
Laurent Giles & Partners	
Built:	1960
A.H. Moody & Son Ltd.	
Owner:	Dr. F. E. Ellis
	U.S.A.

This yacht was one of three built at the Company. Lobie II was built in 1960 for a Major K.G. Wily of Cheshire. One other called Micia was built for Conte. Dott. Raimondo Visconti di Modroni. They were all auxiliary cutters fitted with 4 cylinder 30 BHP Thorneycroft diesel engines. They were of a centre cockpit design with an open wheel house arrangement. They were teak planked with teak laid decks, teak deck work. A serious long distance cruising yacht. Dr. F. E. Ellis of the U.S.A. was to purchase another Laurent Giles design yacht from Moody's in 1972. She was 50'9" LOA. Her hull was of aluminium manufactured by Walter Hewsman of Holland and fitted out to the highest standard at Swanwick. She had teak laid decks and teak deckwork.

Rhiannon

LOA:	32'6"
LWL:	30'6"
Beam:	10'0"
Draft:	3'6"
Thames meas.:	12 tons
Designer:	Frederick R. Parker
	MINA
Built:	1959
A.H. Moody & Son Ltd.	
Lloyds +100:	A1 class
Owner:	Major R.B.
Ramsden *MBE*, Surrey	

Photo from David Moody collection.

The Swanwick motor cruiser was first shown to the public at the London National Boat Show in January 1959. She is intended to be a standard boat which can be produced at a reasonable cost. She can be built to Lloyds supervision and classed if the purchaser is prepared to pay the Society fees. The prototype boat is fitted with the new Perkins Four/ 99 diesel engines and a speed to 10/12 knots is expected. Many other alternative engines, petrol or diesel can be fitted. Careful planning of the accommodation has produced results not obtained in many larger boats. The Swanwick cruiser is adaptable to various layouts but the prototype has a double sleeping cabin forward, galley to port with cooker and sink and a toilet to starboard. The engines are situated under the spacious centre wheelhouse. Adequate seating and an emergency berth on the starboard side After the engine space is the saloon with fitted lockers, table, and full length settee berths. Accommodation is provided for sleeping 4/5/ people. A cockpit is provided aft. She is fitted with electric lighting throughout and is a craft of pleasing appearance to our usual high class finish.

Specification: Includes laminated mahogany stem, mahogany keel, Canadian rock elm hog. Mahogany transom, silver spruce gunnels and stringers, Canadian rock elm timbers, mahogany planking and Afrimosa deck. Blakes toilet, cooking stove, steering wheel mounted on bulkhead. Fuel capacity 70 gallons, water capacity 70 gallons. Bronze stern gear and rudders.

The basic price of this twin screw Swanwick cruiser is £7350 and in this price is allowed a sum of £125 for upholstery and carpets.

One sister ship, Le Cygne, (owned by Mr E.J. Holder of Southampton) was built in 1961. This was fitted with the same engine as Rhiannon.

Extras: Lloyds classification fee - £250: Chromium plating £30: Universal major compass £27.10/-: 1- 2.5" (additional) whale bilge pump £14. 5/-: Search light £8: Electric claxon horn £7. 15/-: Windscreen wiper £6. 6/-: One additional anchor £10. 12. 6d. *Please note: prices shown are those quoted in the early Sixties, and are not relevant today!*

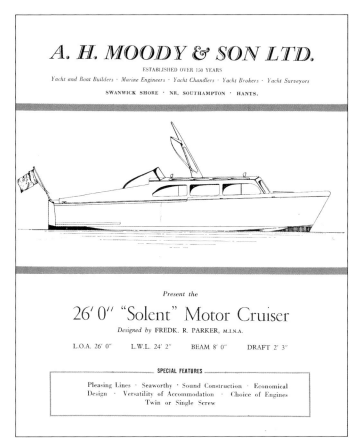

A. H. MOODY & SON LTD.
ESTABLISHED OVER 150 YEARS
Yacht and Boat Builders · Marine Engineers · Yacht Chandlers · Yacht Brokers · Yacht Surveyors
SWANWICK SHORE · NR. SOUTHAMPTON · HANTS.

Present the
26′ 0″ "Solent" Motor Cruiser
Designed by FREDK. R. PARKER, M.I.N.A.

L.O.A. 26′ 0″   L.W.L. 24′ 2″   BEAM 8′ 0″   DRAFT 2′ 3″

——— SPECIAL FEATURES ———

Pleasing Lines · Seaworthy · Sound Construction · Economical
Design · Versatility of Accommodation · Choice of Engines
Twin or Single Screw

Joannah

LOA:	26'0"
LWL:	24'2"
Beam:	8'6"
Draft:	2'3"
Thames meas.:	6 tons
Lloyds +100:	A1 class
Designer:	Frederick R. Parker
	MINA
Built:	1959
A.H. Moody & Son Ltd.	
Owner:	
	Basil C.S. Hordern
	West Sussex

The Solent motor cruiser was first presented to the public at the 1958 National Boat Show and has proved popular. It is understood that 6 were built. She is of a standard design capable of economic production but sound and seaworthy. The Solent can be adapted in several ways to meet the needs of the various purchasers. She can be produced in 4 berth, 3 berth or 2 berth variations, or a sports fishing version. The 4 berth version has proved most popular and this can be produced in a twin or single screw form. Various British engines are suitable as are engines of American manufacture. The boats built in Great Britain have had in the main Parsons Ford Scampi engines, for both twin and single screw. The engines give about 30 HP each and give a speed of 8/9 knots for single screw and 10/11 for twin screw. Great care has been taken over the design and layout and the Solent has the amount of space usually found in far larger boats.

Specification: She has full capacity for 20 gallons of water and 20 gallons of fuel. Electric light is provided throughout and navigation lamps. Her specification includes laminated mahogany stem, mahogany keel, Canadian Rock elm hog, resin bonded plywood transom, mahogany gunnels, silver spruce stringers, double skinned mahogany bottom, resin bonded plywood topsides and deck. She is complete with Baby Blakes toilet. Galley with cooking stove, wheel steering and windscreen, bronze stern gear and rudders. The price of the single screw Solent with Parsons Scampi engine is £2450 at our Yard and the twin screw Solent with the Scampi engines is £2982 at our Yard. Prices for hulls only or boat in any state of completion gladly given.

Two sister ships were built, *Lady Winsome in 1959 (owned by Lt Col D Russell Naylor of Wimbledon Common),* and *Blue Seal, in 1960 (owned by Frederick R. Parker of Warsash).* Both were fitted with twin screw engines. There were six built in total. *Please note: The prices and brochure shown are those used in the late Fifties, early Sixties and are not relevant today!*

Photo from David Moody collection.

Silver Spray

LOA:	32'6"
LWL:	29'0"
Beam:	10'6"
Draft:	2'9"
Built:	1960
A.H. Moody & Son Ltd.	
Owner:	B.K. Taylor

Shown at the London Boat Show 1960.

Powered by 2 x 3 cylinder 100BHP Rootes Lister diesels. Designed by Cox & Haswell Ltd.

Lady Christabel

LOA:	38'3"
LWL:	35'3"
Beam:	9'8"
Draft:	3'0"
Thames meas.:	14 tons
Built:	1938
A.H. Moody & Son Ltd.	
Owner:	
	Sir Morris Jenks
	former Lord Mayor
	of London

Photo from David Moody collection.

Powered by 2 x 4 cylinder Morris petrol engines. Designed by F. Shepherd.

Requisitioned by the Admiralty to take part in the Dunkirk evacuation. Carried out her task and returned safely.

Please note: Build date out of sequence.

Varen

LOA:	41'6"
LWL:	31'6"
Beam:	10'6"
Draft:	6.3"
Sail area:	708 sq.ft.
Thames meas.:	15 tons
Lloyds +100:	A1 Lloyds
Designed by:	G.L. Watson & Co.
Built:	1961
A.H. Moody & Son Ltd.	
Yard No:	411
Owner:	
	Maj. M.S.B. Vernon
	MVO
	Gloucestershire

Photo from David Moody collection.

Photo from David Moody collection.

Varen was built to a very high specification and was the only G.L. Watson design to be built by A.H. Moody & Son Ltd. The photograph shows her launching in May 1961 and Harry Harding is standing on the aft deck. He was to become the new construction foreman. Varen stayed under the same ownership for a good number of years and her rig was changed from a wooden mast and spars to aluminium.

Specification: Teak planking, oak frames, American elm timbers, oak stern post, teak stem, teak deck work and teak laid decks. Lead keel.

Photo by Beken of Cowes

Martinus

LOA:	61'6"
LWL:	55'3"
Beam:	15'9"
Draft:	6'6"
Sail area:	1100 sq.ft.
Thames meas.:	55 tons
Lloyds +100:	A1 class
Designer:	Frederick R. Parker
Built:	1962 A.H. Moody & Son Ltd.
Yard number:	416
Owner:	J.R.P. Martin Surrey

Martinus was one of the largest timber yachts to be built by the company. She was a serious motor sailer for long distance cruising, with a deck saloon and separate aft wheelhouse. She was built and supervised to Lloyds and classified +100 A1. She was also winner of the Lloyds Trophy for the best boat built to Lloyds rules in 1962. She was powered by a 6 cylinder 127 BHP Gardner diesel engine. She had mahogany planked topsides, teak laid deck and teak deck work, hollow silver spruce mast and spars and a ketch rig. She had portholes for extra ventilation in her topsides and her anchor was stowed 'big ships style' in a hosier in forward topside as can be seen in photograph. A classic yacht in all respects.

Killicrankie

LOA:	35'6"
LWL:	26'6"
Beam:	9'6"
Draft:	6'0"
Sail area:	492 sq.ft.
Thames meas.:	10 tons
Lloyds +100:	A1 class
Designer:	Frederick R. Parker *MRINA*
Built:	1962 A.H. Moody & Son Ltd.
Yard number:	415
Owner:	Mr Bruce Kilpatrick Southampton
Price when new:	£9,040

Photo by Beken of Cowes

Killicrankie can be seen in this photograph in full cruising trim with dinghy stowed on the coach roof and helmsman concentrating on the set of the sails.

Accommodation: The accommodation layout makes the most of the space available and will sleep five in comfort. The layout, from forward, consists of a chain locker with shelf over, foc'sle with 2 fixed berths to port and starboard. Aft, on port side, is the toilet, wash basin and cupboard. Opposite on starboard is hanging space. The saloon has 2 settee berths, one to port and one to starboard and a fixed table to the centre with bottle store. There are cupboards, shelves and lockers. Aft on starboard is the well appointed galley with stove, sink and plate stowage etc. On port side there is a quarter berth with chart table over. The engine is sited under the companionway steps and cockpit. There is a self draining cockpit with wheel steering. She has light oak interior finish with electric lighting and navigation lights.

Specification: Ballast keel, lead. Wood keel mahogany. Stem, sternpost, horn timbers, stern knee, false keel and transom all mahogany. Rudder mahogany with bronze main piece. Planking mahogany topsides with teak below the waterline. Timbers are oak bent. Shelf, stringers, beams and beam clamps silver spruce. Main deck teak. Coach roof deck marine plywood. Deck work, hatches and combings etc in teak. Mast and spars silver spruce. Sails terylene by Tratman and Lowther, Bristol. Freshwater 40 gallons. Fuel 18 gallons. Engine a Parsons Scampi direct drive 4 cylinder 10/24 BHP petrol engine. There is stowage on the coach roof for a 7'6" dinghy.

Photo from Southern Daily Echo.

Killicrankie was shown at the London International Boat Show in 1962 with the kind permission of her owner, Mr Bruce Kilpatrick. I wanted to make contact again with this client as his family had a long standing relationship with our company. Having located Mr. Kilpatrick, we decided to meet at the Royal Lymington Yacht Club over lunch, and then to his home. Mr. Kilpatrick was obviously very comfortable dealing with Moody as he was to purchase four boats from us over the years. It could have been his loyalty to the company or the fact that we were producing the products that he aspired to at the time that caused him to stay with us as a client. Killicrankie, like all Mr. Kilpatrick's boats, were kept and maintained to a very high standard. Because of this they retained their value and at that time were a form of investment as I have already mentioned.

The yacht was to be extensively cruised in British and French waters by the family and Mr. Kilpatrick reflected on a passage that he made from the Solent to Brixham in increasing severe weather conditions. He explains the yacht stood by him extremely well and he felt safe. There was apparently one other yacht built by Moody on the same passage and she was Moonspray with Mrs. Lee Duncan at the helm.

Killicrankie was sold in 1967 as Mr. Kilpatrick wanted to try motor boating and the new material called GRP (Glass Reinforced Plastic). It also required less annual maintenance. He chose a design by Graham Moody called the Lancer 42, which was moulded by the Tyler Boat Company and fitted out at our yard at Swanwick to a high standard of internal finish. She was named Loch Tummel and was a displacement twin screw motor yacht. Loch Tummel was shown at the Earls Court Boat Show in 1968. Mr. Kilpatrick was to own this boat for ten years before selling her to a client who departed to the Mediterranean. She was extensively cruised and loved by the Kilpatrick family.

Photo from David Moody collection.

Photo from D.B.L. Imaging.

His third yacht saw the Kilpatrick family return to sailing. Kilcreggan, was a centre cockpit Moody 42 ketch designed by the late Angus Primrose, moulded by Robert Ives Ltd. and finished at Swanwick. There were two versions built on this hull - a deck saloon version with aft cockpit, which tended to be more popular at the time and a centre cockpit version which was very deep and reassuring and gave you tremendous protection from the elements as there was an open wheel house arrangement over. Her accommodation below was very large for the time and was the accommodation of a larger yacht. Angus seemed to have the skill of producing a design which was a good compromise between performance and accommodation. The photograph shows the Moody 42 in full sail. The 42s were fitted out to a high standard and with a modern style of joinery, mainly of teak and teak veneer. She again was well used and maintained.

Kilcreggan was sold in mid-1983. Following this, Mr. Kilpatrick purchased a second hand Moody 36, Carancho, designed by Angus Primrose and built by Marine Projects at Plymouth. She was of an open cockpit design with a sloop rig, of similar design era as Kilcreggan, following similar hull design trends.

1993 saw Mr. Kilpatrick's fourth purchase. It was to be a Moody 35 to a Bill Dixon design. She was centre cockpit sloop, and was named Kilmory. This boat had very attractive lines and looks right from the outside and good accommodation below decks including a passageway between the saloon and the aft cabin. Kilmory was eventually sold in 1997. Photo shows a similar Moody 35.

Mr. Kilpatrick dealt with a number of family members, starting with my father. I was lucky to have dealt with this client on a number of occasions. He was both honourable but fair and firm. His boats were always kept in outstanding condition which made our lives a lot easier when coming to sell them second hand. GRP in the early days seemed to come with its own problems and invariably adjustments had to be made in price when selling second hand.

It was pleasure to meet with Mr. Kilpatrick again to chat about the boats he owned and his connection with the family. He continues to be interested in boating.

Photo by Beken of Cowes

Maenad

LOA:	41'8"
LWL:	31'3"
Beam:	10'1"
Draft:	6'8"
Sail area:	700 sq.ft.
Thames meas.:	13 tons
Lloyds +100:	A1 class
Designer:	Frederick R. Parker *MINA*
Built:	1962 A.H. Moody & Son Ltd.
Yard no:	417
Owner:	Mrs N.B.M. St. C. Malleson, Warsash

Piscis of Towy

LOA:	37'9"
LWL:	35'8"
Beam:	11'0"
Draft:	4'0"
Sail area:	410 sq.ft.
Thames meas.:	16 tons
Lloyds +100:	A1 class
Designer:	Frederick R.Parker *MINA*
Built:	1963 A.H. Moody & Son Ltd.
Yard no:	420
Owner:	Major T.V. Fisher-Hoch Carmarthenshire

Photo from David Moody collection.

Photo by Beken of Cowes

Melita

LOA:	58'3"
LWL:	53'6"
Beam:	14'0"
Draft:	4'8"
Sail area:	420 sq.ft.
Thames meas.:	46 tons
Lloyds +100:	A1 class
Designer:	Laurent Giles & Partners
Built:	1963, A.H. Moody & Son Ltd.
Yard number:	424
Owner:	Wg Cdr R.G. Grant-Ferris MP, London

The design brief was to design and build a boat with comfort that was capable of cruising in deep water and through the canals of Europe, therefore her draft and air draft were to be as low as possible. She was primarily a twin screw diesel yacht with substantial steadying sails. Her masts were placed in tabernacles so they could be lowered and the wheel house was detachable so as to reduce air draft when confronted with low bridges. She was powered by twin 6 cylinder 106 BHP Gardner diesel engines. She had teak deck work and teak laid decks. A classic motor yacht built for a specific purpose.

Photo from David Moody collection.

Photo by Beken of Cowes

Donzella

LOA:	33'9"
LWL:	30'7"
Beam:	10'8"
Draft:	2'9"
Thames meas.:	13 tons
Designer:	Frederick R. Parker
	MINA
Built:	1965
A.H. Moody & Son Ltd.	
Owner: Mr & Mrs M.A.	
Taylor, Reading	

With the ever increasing demand for powerboats, Donzella was designed and produced to make a standard class of a moderately fast powerboat. On sea trials she achieved in the order of 15 to 16 knots. She was of the "Tormentor Class" as she was built on the old site of HMS Tormentor at Warsash which Moody owned at the time. She was shown at the 1965 London International Boat Show.

Accommodation: From forward, chain locker, foc'sle with two fitted single berths - one to port and starboard. Lockers under and wardrobes. The main saloon had a double dinette arrangement to port, after this was the L-shaped galley with stove, fridge and sink. On starboard was a extendable settee berth with lockers, bookcase etc. After this was the W.C. compartment. She had a large open cockpit with a covered steering position. Her engines were mounted under the cockpit floor. She was powered by twin Perkins 120BHP diesel engines. Her construction was of a multistringer principle with seven stringers per side. She was of mahogany planking on steam bent timbers.

Photo by Beken of Cowes

Firedancer

LOA:	41'7"
LWL:	30'0"
Beam:	10'7"
Draft:	6'6"
Sail area:	700 sq.ft.
Thames meas.:	16 tons
Lloyds +100:	A1 class
Designer:	C.R. Holman
Built:	1965
A.H. Moody & Son Ltd.	
Yard number:	428
Owner:	
D.S. & Mrs. E.R. Cottell	
	Old Bursledon

Firedancer and her sistership, Mabel Amelia, were built in consecutive years and would have been of similar specification. The topsides would have been of mahogany splined planking, and teak planking below the waterline. Her timbers and frames would have been of elm with teak laid decks and teak deck work. Wheel steering and a self draining cockpit. She was powered by a 47 HP 4 cylinder Perkins diesel engine. A real classic looking yacht with pleasing lines. Looked after, this yacht would last several lifetimes.

Firedancer was shown at the 1965 London Boat Show and ran away with the Boat of the Show Award. Mabel Amelia was owned by Capt. D.E. & B.C. McManus (Ret) from Harpenden, and classed at Lloyds +100A1.

Photo by Beken of Cowes

Josephine VII

LOA:	36'0"
LWL:	25'6"
Beam:	9'6"
Draft:	6'0"
Sail area:	550 sq.ft.
Designer:	Sparkman & Stephens Inc
Built:	1965 A.H. Moody & Son Ltd.
Yard number:	430
Owner:	Cosby Smallpiece Swanwick Shore

Josephine VII was the last of Mr. Smallpiece's racing yachts. She was of the Hestia design from the drawing board of Sparkman and Stephens and was the fore-runner to the One Ton Cup series. She was designed with a long keel and a triangular shaped rudder. You often saw two people at the wheel fighting to hold her course on down wind legs. She was incredibly quick for her time and won many races inshore and offshore. The next design from Sparkman and Stephens had a radical new shape below the water line called a 'fin and skeg'. Two boats were built on the Isle of Wight called 'Roundabout and Clarionet' and were to take most of the honours for the foreseeable future. Her method of construction was also different being glued on edge planking. This was new technology and temperature for curing of the glue was very important. As far as I can recall, she was mahogany planking with mahogany deck work and canvas covered decks. Large self draining cockpit and wheel steering. Aluminium masts and spars. She had a 2 cylinder, 12 HP Arona diesel engine which was very light weight for a diesel.

Larne

LOA:	49'0"
LWL:	38'0"
Beam:	12'2"
Draft:	7'0"
Sail area:	1100 sq.ft.
Thames meas.:	23 tons
Lloyds +100:	A1 class
Designer:	Frederick R. Parker *MINA*
Built: A.H. Moody & Son Ltd.	1965
Yard number:	431
Owner:	R.A. Marryat, London

Photo by Beken of Cowes

Larne was extensively cruised in European waters and much loved by her original owner. During Mr. Marryat's ownership, she had been stolen but returned safely with little damage. She was missing for quite some time though. I was fortunate in crewing on this boat with my brother when I was in my late teens. We joined the boat in Alicante and our first passage was to Ibiza, then on to Majorca, Minorca, Sardinia and Pantelleria Island before arriving in the old harbour in Valetta, Malta. I gained a lot of experience on this trip as there were only three of us on board. Our watches were in the order of four hours on and two hours off during the night. This would consist of 2 hours on the helm, 2 hours on watch and 2 hours in the bunk. The other two people on board were the owner and an ex-skipper of the yacht Lutine, belonging to Lloyds the insurance underwriters. My brother had left the boat in the Ballyerics. I flew home from Malta, I remember, in a BOAC Comet 4.

Larne was to be sold in 1975 to Dougal Robertson who became famous with his family for writing the true story 'Survive the Savage Sea' which told of his frightening experience when his yacht Lucette was sunk in June 1972 following an attack from a killer whale. He spent 38 days at sea in a life raft before being sighted and rescued. The book is a very gripping read. He left the yard bound for Hong Kong.

Larne was built to a very high specification. She had varnished teak planking topsides with a teak laid deck, teak deck work, lead keel and a Perkins 27 BHP 4 cylinder diesel engine. Wheel steering and hollow silver spruce mast and spars. Her build was supervised by Lloyds and classed +100 A1. She also won the Lloyds Trophy for best yacht built under Lloyds classification that year. All in all she was a wonderful yacht.

Spring Dawn

Photo by Beken of Cowes

LOA:	28'6"
LWL:	25'6"
Beam:	10'6"
Draft:	1'9"
Thames meas.:	11 tons
Designer:	Frederick R Parker *MRINA*
Built:	1966 A.H. Moody & Son Ltd.
Owner:	Mr P. C. Wadham Emsworth

Spring Dawn was a twin screw sports cruiser built at the Warsash yard.

Accommodation: From aft: a large aft cockpit with sunbathing area. An attractively laid out steering position with helmsman and passenger seats. Six foot head room throughout the main accommodation. Four sleeping berths, a spacious galley with ample working space. Toilet compartment has a shower and washbasin. An open plan saloon with a raised dinette.

Specification: Stem and keel laminated mahogany. Transom mahogany 10/88 ply. Planking double skin bottom and seam and batten topsides. Frames mahogany, cockpit and main decks teak laid, deck work and combings teak. Coachwork top ply Casco sheathed. Bulkheads 10/88 ply. Morse steering. Fuel tank 120 gallons. Water tank 30 gallons. Powered by 2 x Volvo Penta 150 HP petrol engines with Volvo Penta 200 outdrives with electric lifts.

Other equipment: 17lb anchor; 25 fathoms of ¼ inch short link chain; 2 x 20 fathoms 1½ inch Terylene mooring warps; 2 horseshoe type lifebuoys; 1 Grabit type boat hook Boarding ladder; 2 fire extinguishers; stainless steel pulpit and stanchions.

Firedancer of Hamble

LOA:	47'0"
LWL:	37'0"
Beam:	13'3"
Draft:	6'10"
Sail area:	754 sq.ft.
Thames meas.:	20 tons
Lloyds +100:	A1 class
Designed by:	Frederick R. Parker *MRINA*
Built:	1968 A.H. Moody & Son Ltd.
Yard No:	445
Owner:	D.S. Cottell Old Bursledon

Photo from David Moody collection.

Firedancer of Hamble was the second yacht to be built for this owner. She was a true deck saloon with owner stateroom aft.

Accommodation: From forward, chain locker, foc'sle with berth to port, stowage to starboard. Aft to forward cabin with 2 bunks to port and 2 bunks to starboard. After this was a toilet compartment with shower and hot and cold pressurised water system. Aft and up to the deck saloon with good all round visibility. Aft of this was the owner's stateroom with generous single berths with en suite WC with shower, hot and cold pressurised water system. Opposite was wardrobe and cupboard space.

Specification: Powered by a Perkins 4/236 diesel engine 71 BHP with 2:1 reduction gear. She has a 400 mile range under power at a good cruising speed. 150 gallons of fuel, 100 gallons of water. Her mast and spars were aluminium by Proctor and her steering gear was Rod by Mathway. She had teak laid decks and teak deck work and her internal finish was in teak and mahogany. Her main wheel steering position was on the bridge deck with a small windscreen forward.

Photo by Beken of Cowes

Swan Dancer

LOA:	53'0"
LWL:	45'0"
Beam:	14'0"
Draft:	6'6"
Sail area:	947 sq.ft.
Thames meas.:	37 tons
Lloyds +100:	A1 class
Designer:	Frederick R. Parker
Built:	1970 A.H. Moody & Son Ltd.
Yard number:	458
Owner:	P.W. Allsebrook Sussex

Swan Dancer was the last private timber yacht to be built at Swanwick. I was lucky enough to experience the build and put my skills into practice. She was of modern concept being fin and skeg configuration which made her more manoeuvrable under power. She was a true motor sailer with a deck saloon with bridge deck steering and also under cover steering. With ketch rig configuration, it made her an exceptional cruising boat. She was powered by a 6 cylinder 195 BHP Leyland diesel engine. She was constructed of mahogany

Photograph from Ajaxnetphoto.com

planking topsides and iroko planking below waterline. On mainly iroko stem, frames and stern post. Lead ballast. Teak deck work and teak laid decks. Aluminium mast and spars.

To Commemorate the Launching
by
Elizabeth Allsebrook

on Saturday, 20th June, 1970

of

𝒮wan 𝒟ancer

DESIGNED BY **FREDERICK R. PARKER** M.R.I.N.A.

AND BUILT AT MOODY'S YARD, SWANWICK

UNDER THE DIRECTION OF **MR. GORDON MOODY**

AND SUPERVISION OF **MR. JIM SAUNDERS**

FOR LLOYD'S CLASSIFICATION ✠ 100A1 ✠ LMC

BY THE FOLLOWING

Managers, Foremen & Chargehands

GRAHAM MOODY	HARRY HARDING	PAT WILLCOCKS	REG. MUDD
BOB SNELGAR	BILL BOURNE	STAN RENDLE	LIONEL WILLSHER
JACK BENNETT	DOUG. POOLE	RALPH NORFOLK	

Shipwrights

B. C. NOTT	H. WORSFOLD	T. WELLSTEAD	I. BLOW
A. R. NORTON	A. DOE	A. MERRITT	T. J. RICHARDS
	R. HEASELL	D. HOPKINS	

Joiners

C. HARDING	W. BLOW	R. MEARS	A. BOYES
M. RUDGLEY	J. BOYES	K. MOORE	J. FERN

Fitters

E. WATTS	R. TURNER	J. H. EDWARDS	R. P. FORD

Painters

H. H. JONES	D. W. LEPPARD	J. DAVEY	F. STAMP

Electrician

B. R. LEWIS

Apprentices

A. P. HOWARD	D. PRENTICE	V. C. SIMMONDS	R. MAY
R. SHAWYER	S. J. CHALMERS	S. TITLEY	N. PALMER
R. W. COLE	D. A. MOODY	A. SNOOK	E. PARSONS
D. WRIGHT	K. B. WHITTEN	I. SHARP	P. ROGERS

Photo by Beken of Cowes

Morning Cloud

LOA:	43.9'
LWL:	36.8'
Beam:	13.3'
Draft:	7.8'
Tons:	17.87 tons
Sail number:	2468
Designed by:	Ron Holland
Hull and deck by:	Maitland Marine Ltd Aluminium Alloy
Fitted out by:	A.H. Moody & Son Ltd. 1977
Yard number:	577
Owner:	Rt. Hon. Edward Heath *MBE MP*

This was to be the last in a long line of Morning Clouds that had been successfully campaigned and raced to represent Great Britain in many International events.

The hull and deck was manufactured by Maitland Marine of Woking and fitted out at Swanwick. Her mast and spars were by Proctor Metal Masts.

Deadlines had to be met as she was required to take part in selection trials for the Admirals Cup in 1977. The mast was rigged and stepped by Spencers of Cowes and the sails supplied by North Sails (UK) Ltd. Unfortunately she was not selected as part of the winning British Admirals Cup team of 1977 but managed to be selected in 1979 along with Blizzard and Eclipse to represent Britain, having had major modifications to the stern sections which made her a quicker boat. The team finished 6th. In one of the races, Morning Cloud had broken her carbon fibre rudder and had to return to the Hamble to fit a spare aluminium one. This had an effect on Britain's

Rt. Hon. Edward Heath.
Photograph from Ajaxnetphoto.com

chances. It was during this year that the Fastnet race was hit by a freak storm in the western approaches. It was a storm that killed 19 people and all but four were taking part in the Fastnet race. The crew on board Morning Cloud all returned safely albeit shaken by the experience. Her crew included Owen Parker (sailing master), Peter Bateman (tactician) and Larry Marks (helmsman). Our own Christopher Moody was also part of this crew. Photo on the right shows the Rt. Hon. Edward Heath aboard Morning Cloud at her launching May 1st 1977.

Glass Reinforced Plastic (GRP) Yachts

1965-1989

VIOLANTE

This section illustrates a selection of GRP yachts fitted out or built by Moody,

Carbineer 44 and the Cavalier 36 being shown at the London International Boat Show, Earls Court 1970.
Photo from Ajaxnetphoto.com.

Salar 40

Salar 40 class

LOA:	39'0"
LWL:	31'0"
Beam:	11'3"
Draft:	5'3"
Sail area:	
	sloop 670 sq.ft.
	ketch 640 sq.ft.
Thames meas.:	19 tons
Designer:	
Laurent Giles & Partners	
Moulded by:	
	Kemp & Pitt Ltd
Fitted out by:	
	A H Moody & Son Ltd
Built:	
Duration: 1965-1967	
Number built:	7
	2 wood, 5 GRP

Photo from David Moody collection.

The first two Salar 40s were built in timber at our yard in Swanwick. Five more GRP versions were fitted out at our Warsash Yard for Salterns Yacht Agency Ltd. She was a true motor sailer with the engine mounted below the centre cockpit. She had an open wheel house with centrally mounted steering at the forward end of cockpit. Her aft cabin was accessed from the cockpit. Tunnels between the forward and aft accommodation had not yet been introduced. She was an attractive, full bodied yacht that met the compromise between good spacious accommodation whilst still maintaining those classic Laurent Giles cruising boat lines.

Accommodation: From forward: Chain locker. Forward cabin with 2 fitted single berths. Aft on port is the well fitted toilet compartment. Aft of this is a double dinette arrangement with locker and cupboards. Opposite on starboard is a wardrobe and well appointed galley with stove, sink, fridge/ice box. Aft of galley is the wet locker. Passing up into the cockpit and into the aft cabin you have a wardrobe to starboard and a second WC to port with 2 fitted single berths, one to port and one to starboard.

She was powered by a Perkins 4.236M 50BHP diesel engine with 150 gallons of fuel in 2 wing tanks fitted beneath the cockpit floor. This would give her a range under power of approximately 1000 miles cruising between 6 and 7 knots. 100 gallons of fresh water mounted centrally under saloon.

Halberdier 36

LOA:	36'1"
LWL:	28'0"
Beam:	11'1"
Draft:	5'0"
Sail area:	
	sloop 703 sq.ft.
	ketch 611 sq.ft.
Thames meas.:	15.2 tons
Lloyds +100:	A1 class
Designer:	Alan F. Hill
Moulded by:	
	Marine Construction
	(Woolston) Ltd
Fitted out and marketed by:	
	A.H. Moody & Son Ltd.
First boats when new:	
	£13,000
Build duration:	
	1967-1973
Number built:	31

Photograph shows Alerica under full sail. The Halberdier was fitted out at Swanwick and the hull and deck was moulded at Marine Construction at Woolston. The Halberdier was distinctive as the majority were moulded with a white hull and grey superstructure with the Heraldic symbol of a Halberd embossed either side of her bows. There were 29 Halberdiers built at Swanwick and a number of part assemblies sold for self completion. Photo by Beken of Cowes.

Accommodation: From forward: Chain locker, fore cabin with two fixed berths - one to port and one to starboard. Aft to port was the toilet compartment and hanging space opposite on starboard. Saloon with a U shaped settee to port, with a unique table that stowed away allowing this area to be made into a large berth. Out board of this, on port, was a pilot berth. Opposite on starboard was a galley with gimballed stove, sink and fridge with chart table over. The galley was well appointed and had cutlery, crockery and food storage. Also the saloon had a number of lockers and cupboards. Up into the centre cockpit with open wheelhouse over, steering to forward port side with 2 benches port and starboard. Entering into aft cabin with second toilet compartment to starboard with two fixed staggered berths port and starboard to allow for external lazarett locker.

The interior finish was of heavily grain patterned mahogany. She was powered by a Perkins 4108 with a 2-1 reduction gear box, flexibly mounted diesel engine. 100 gallons of fuel and 90 gallons fresh water. She came standard with 2 Delux Baby Blakes toilets, refrigerator, hot and cold pressurised water system via a Valliant 125 multipoint water heater. Shower. Electric power points and lighting to all cabins. Self draining cockpit. Mathway steering. Moulded to Lloyds 100A1. Teak trim on deck. External iron keel. Deck structure fully insulated throughout. Mast sound deadened and anodised aluminium.

Cavalier 36

LOA:	36'1"
LWL:	28'0"
Beam:	11'1"
Draft:	5'0"
Sail area:	572 sq.ft.
Thames meas.:	13 tons
Designed by:	Alan F. Hill
Moulded by:	Marine Construction Woolston Ltd
Fitted out and marketed by:	A.H. Moody & Son Ltd.
Build duration:	1970-1972
Number built:	8

Photo by Beken of Cowes.

The Cavalier 36 was a derivative of the Halberdier 36, using the same hull but fitted with a different deck assembly, generally moulded in a distinctive light blue hull with cream decks. They were a deck saloon configuration with an aft cockpit and external wheel steering position. A Bermudan sloop rig, powered by a Perkins 4107, 4 cylinder 35 BHP diesel engine. Again the hull and superstructure was moulded by Marine Construction at Woolston and designed by Alan F. Hill. A total of 8 boats were built. Production was introduced in 1970 and ceased in 1972.

Accommodation: From forward: Chain locker. Forecabin with 2 fitted berths - one port, one starboard. Aft, the WC compartment with shower, toilet and basin on portside and wardrobe on starboard. Moving aft, there is a large cabin with a single berth on the starboard side and a double berth on the port side which includes a small dressing table and wardrobe forward. Moving up and aft, you enter the deck saloon which measures some 8' x 8'. The well appointed galley is situated on the starboard side and an L shaped settee on the port side. Moving into the large open aft cockpit, with seating and wheel steering.

Carbineer 44/46

LOA:	44'0"
LWL:	36'0"
Beam:	12'2"
Draft:	6'0"
Sail area:	
	ketch 850 sq.ft.
Thames meas.:	22 tons
Lloyds + 100	A1 class
Designer:	
Laurent Giles & Partners	
Moulded by:	
Marine Construction (Woolston) Ltd.	
Fitted out and marketed by:	
A.H. Moody & Son Ltd.	
Build duration:	
	1969 - 1979
Number built:	32

One of the first references to the Carbineer or Carabin (the word is of Spanish origin) is the establishment of a troop of Carbine and pistol equipped Light Cavalry in 1559 by Henry II of France. By 1630 the Carbine had been standardised in England to a length of 45" while further editions including a sliding bar and ring were made during the 18th century for shoulder attachment. Ironically with the demise of the horse the modern Carbine has reverted to its original status, that of an Infantry weapon. (Original brochure quote). This is how the Carbineer 44 motor sailer derived its name. Photo by Beken of Cowes.

The Carbineer 44 was introduced to the market in 1969 and appeared at the London International Boat Show in the same year. She instantly won acclaim as a deck saloon motor sailer with aft cockpit steering and internal steering. Her underwater shape was of modern concept with a fin and skeg configuration and fitted standard with a ketch rig. The photograph shows her sailing prowess. Designed by Laurent Giles & Partners and the hull and deck mouldings being manufactured by Marine Construction at Woolston and fitted out at Swanwick. The interior was mostly of teak and teak laminate. Externally, the fibreglass was broken up with the use of teak capping rails, teak hatches and teak combings to the saloon. She had a teak aft cockpit grating and teak laid decks were supplied as an option. She had aluminium mast and spars. In 1973 she became the Carbineer 46. This was achieved by straightening the stem by 6 inches and extending the transom aft by approximately 18 inches to 2 feet.

Deck saloon looking forward. Photo from David Moody collection.

Carbineer 44/46 (cont)

As the Carbineer 44 was semi-custom, there were a number of accommodation options available with the ability to move some non-structural bulkheads. The carbineer was powered by a 6 cylinder Perkins 6354 Marine diesel engine, 95BHP. This was flexibly mounted under the saloon floor with fuel tanks to port and starboard with water tanks mounted forward and between the fuel tanks. Fuel capacity was 220 gallons, water capacity 180 gallons. The shaft was fitted with a brake to stop the prop turning whilst under sail. She was fitted with two WC compartments which included shower, toilet and basin. Hot and cold pressurized water system to galley and both WC compartments. Large self draining cockpit. She was supplied standard with the following: Calor gas cooker, refrigerator in gas or electric, two banks of batteries, a 240 volt ring main with 13 amp socket outlet in each cabin. Deck wash and hose, upholstery, carpets and curtains, stern davits, side screens and sail coats. Two fenders, boat hook and bucket. Production ceased after ten years in 1979 with 32 Carbineers having been built.

Carbineer 46. Photo from D.B.L. Imaging.

Photo by Beken of Cowes.

Lancer 42

LOA:	42'6"
LWL:	38'6"
Beam:	12'7"
Draft:	3'7"
Thames meas.:	25 tons
Lloyds +100:	A1 class

Designed by:	Graham A. Moody
Moulded by:	Tyler Boat Company
Fitted out and marketed by:	A.H. Moody & Son Ltd.
Build duration:	1968-1972
Number built:	5 built

Accommodation: From forward, chain locker, foc'sle with 2 'V-berths' (one to port, one to starboard). Aft on port is the toilet compartment including shower and washbasin, with wardrobes opposite. Aft on portside is the saloon with an L-shaped settee with cupboards and book shelves behind. She features the same foldaway table as the Halberdier. Opposite on the starboard side is the fully equipped galley and cocktail cabinet. Up into the wheel house there is seating and second steering position to port side. Moving aft, on port side is a single berth cabin with toilet compartment with shower and washbasin opposite on starboard. Aft stateroom is finished in oak with 2 generous single berths, one to port and one to starboard with dressing table between. The cabin also features large wardrobes and cupboard space.

Specification: Powered by 2x Perkins 6/354 Marine diesels with 2:1 reduction gear boxes. Fuel capacity of approx. 340 gallons and water capacity approx. 200 gallons. She is fitted with 2 Baby Blakes Delux toilets. Pressurised hot and cold water system. 220/240 volt ring main. Carpets, curtains and upholstery. The Lancer is a displacement motor yacht with emphasis on quality and comfort.

The standard engine installation approximate ranges and speeds.

1800 RPM: 9 knots, 720 miles.

2100 RPM: 10 knots 570 miles.

Photo by Beken of Cowes.

Moody 44

LOA:	44'0"
LWL:	34'0"
Beam:	12'7"
Standard draft:	6'6"
Shallow draft:	5'9"
Thames meas.:	22 tons
Sail area: sloop & ketch	1035 sq.ft.
Designer: Laurent Giles	& Partners Ltd.
Moulded by:	Halmatic Ltd.
Fitted out by: A.H. Moody & Son Ltd.	
Build duration:	1972-1975
Number built:	18 built

The Moody 44 design was the result of three years' study with the aid of tank testing. She was developed as a cruiser/racer. She was available in a ketch and a sloop rig and the interior was fitted out in teak. Her decks were teak laid. She had a large, self draining centre cockpit with wheel steering.

Accommodation: From forward: Chain locker. Forward cabin with 2 fitted berths. Forward WC with shower, basin and toilet. Saloon with U shaped settee to port with storage above. A settee berth opposite on starboard with trotter box. Above and out board a pilot berth is provided. A navigation station aft to port including forward facing chart table with full length berth. Opposite on starboard is the galley with work top, gimballed cooker, S/S sink, A passageway on starboard side to aft cabin with another full length berth. Owner's cabin with a berth to port and starboard with an ensuite WC with basin, shower and toilet. Accessible from deck is the lazarett.

Specification: Powered by a 4 cylinder Perkins 4108 40 HP diesel engine or a Thorneycroft 157 62 HP diesel engine. The engine was flexibly mounted under the centre cockpit floor. Fuel capacity 100 gallons. Water capacity 120 gallons. Her keel was incapsulated in GRP and the use of internal glass fibre mouldings were installed as part of the interior structure. She was a very sleek looking yacht. Probably before her time. She had a very straight sheer with her hull deck joint being covered by a teak rubber. She had a distinctive knuckle in her topsides forward which reflected the Laurent Giles style.

Moody 44 (cont)

Photo from D.B.L. Imaging.

The above photograph is the sloop version of the centre cockpit Moody 44. She is shown below with the Carbineer 44 at the London International Boat Show at Earls Court in 1972. This was her first showing at a major international show and was well received.

Photograph from Ajaxnetphoto.com

Moody 42

Mk I & Mk II

LOA:	41'10"
LWL:	34'10"
Beam:	13'4"
Draft:	5'6"
Displacement:	24,200 lbs
Sail area:	762 sq.ft.
Engine:	Perkins 4/236 62 shaft HP
Designed:	Angus S. Primrose
Moulded by:	Robert Ives (Boat Builders) Ltd
Fitted out and marketed by:	A.H. Moody & Son Ltd.
Build duration:	1977-81
Number built:	47

Photo from D.B.L. Imaging.

Photo from D.B.L. Imaging.

The Moody 42 was to be the largest number of any single design to be fitted out at Moody's yard. In four years 47 were built. She was very popular as a cruising yacht as she offered a good compromise between spacious accommodation and sailing performance. The hull and superstructure was of GRP and the hull deck joint was covered by an aluminium toe rail. Teak decks were an option, but many chose the maintenance-free version. She had two steering positions - one aft and one in the saloon. She had aluminium mast and spars. The engine installation is situated under the saloon with easy access through the floor. She was very manoeuvrable under power especially when going astern. Fuel capacity 90 gallons. Water capacity 110 gallons. Accommodation to sleep 8.

Accommodation: From forward: Chain locker, foc'sle with 2 fixed single berths, one to port and one to starboard, wardrobe and cupboards. Aft, on port is a separate twin bunk cabin with wardrobe and dressing table. Opposite is a large WC compartment with wash basin and shower etc. Aft, to the deck saloon on port side is a large U shaped galley. Opposite on starboard is the second steering position. Aft of this is the chart table. On the port side there is a large U shaped settee with table and a small settee opposite on starboard. The aft cabin has a large double berth to starboard and an en suite WC to port including shower, wash basin etc.. Large wardrobe and cupboard space.

Photo from D.B.L. Imaging.

Moody 42 CC

LOA:	41'6"
LWL:	34'2"
Beam:	13'4"
Draft:	5'2"
Thames meas.:	18.52 tons
Sail area:	762 sq.ft.
Engine:	Perkins 4/236 shaft HP
Designed by:	Angus S. Primrose
Moulded by:	Robert Ives (Boat Builders) Ltd
Fitted out and marketed by:	A.H. Moody & Son Ltd.
Build duration:	1978 - 1982
Number built:	7

The Moody 42 centre cockpit was developed using the same hull as the Moody 42 Deck Saloon. There was very often a demand for an open sheltered centre cockpit configuration. The 42 cc featured a very deep centre cockpit and a carefully engineered fibreglass GRP open wheel house. The hull deck joint again was covered by an aluminium toe rail and had all the excellent features of the 42 DS e.g. good manoeuvrability under power and sail and large accommodation with a quality finish. Fuel capacity is 90 gallons. Water capacity 110 gallons. Accommodation to sleep 6 - 8 people.

Accommodation: From forward: chain locker, foc'sle with 2 single fitted berths convertible into a large double plus wardrobe and dressing table to starboard. Aft on port a double guest cabin with upper and lower berths, dressing table and wardrobe. Opposite on starboard a spacious WC compartment with shower and washbasin. Aft into saloon to port is a large U shaped settee with dining table. Opposite on starboard is the chart stowage and table. Aft of this is the galley which is located half in the saloon and passageway to aft cabin. Engine room is accessible from the passageway. The owner's cabin has 2 fitted berths one to port and one to starboard which is convertible to one double. Dressing table, wardrobe and plenty of cupboard space. A spacious en suite WC to port with shower and wash basin. The Centre Cockpit houses the steering position and a large storage locker to port side. Once again the Moody quality is reflected in the internal fit out and joinery.

Moody 63

LOA: 63'0" • *LWL:* 48'0" • *Beam:* 16.5" • *Displacement:* 35/5 tons • *Draft:* (fin) 8'0" • *Sail area:* 1621 sq.ft. (ketch rig) • *Engine:* Perkins 140 HP diesel • *Built:* 1974

Accommodation: to sleep 8 exc. saloon.

Custom built, alternative layouts were offered. Deck saloon. Twin steering positions. Aft cockpit.

Moody 379

LOA: 37'9" • *LWL:* 31'0" • *Beam:* 12'0" • *Draft:* 6'6" • *Displacement:* 14,000 lbs • *Sail area:* 692 sq.ft. • *Engine:* Bukh DV36ME 36 HP diesel • *Build duration:* 1980-1982 • *Designed by:* German Frers • *Moulded by:* Robert Ives Boat builders Ltd. • *Fitted out by:* A.H. Moody & Son Ltd. • *Number built:* 4

Accommodation: to sleep 8 in 3 cabins including saloon.

Aft cockpit performance yacht with wheel steering.

Grenadier 183

LOA: 60'0" • *LWL:* 48'0" • *Beam:* 16'5" • *Draft:* (fin) 8'0" • *Sail area:* 1621 sq.ft. (ketch rig) • *Engine:* Perkins 140 HP diesel • *Built:* 1982

Accommodation: to sleep 8 exc. saloon.

Custom built, alternative layouts were offered. Centre cockpit wheel steering.

The Moody 63 and Grenadier 183 used the same hull with above water modifications designed by Laurent Giles and Partners Ltd, moulded by Halmatic, fitted out by A.H. Moody & Son Ltd. There was also a Moody 66 built using the same hull. The transom was an extended counter stern.

Moody Grenadier 119

LOA: 39'2" • *LWL:* 29'0" • *Beam:* 12'5" • *Draft:* 6'0" • *Displacement:* 9700 lbs • *Sail area:* 759 sq.ft. • *Engine:* Perkins 4.108 47 HP diesel • *Build duration:* 1980 - 1983 • *Designed by:* Laurent Giles & Partners Ltd. • *Moulded and fitted out by:* A.H. Moody & Son Ltd. • *Number Built:* 3

Accommodation: to sleep 6 in 3 cabins incl saloon.

Centre cockpit wheel steering sloop rig.

Moody Grenadier 134

LOA:	44'0"
LWL:	34'6"
Beam:	13'6"
Draft:	(fin keel) 7'0"
Shoal keel:	6'3"
Displacement:	14.5 tons
Sail area:	900 sq.ft.
Engine:	Perkins 4.236 72 HP diesel engine
Designer:	Laurent Giles & Partners Ltd
Build duration:	1980-1986
Number built:	10
Hull moulded by:	Robert Ives (Boat Builders Ltd)
Fitted out and marketed by:	A.H. Moody & Son Ltd, Swanwick

Photo from D.B.L. Imaging.

Another classic centre cockpit design from the drawing board of Laurent Giles and Partners. She was available in ketch rig with a deep keel and a shoal keel. The hull and superstructure was of GRP. The mast and spars were aluminium. There was a large flush deck forward with the coach roof starting aft of the main mast. This may be seen in the photograph. She had teak laid decks over glass fibre and the interior finish was mainly of teak and teak veneer. A high quality deep sea cruising yacht of distinction and character.

Accommodation: From forward, chain locker, foc'sle with 2 fitted single berths, one to port and one to starboard with wardrobes and cupboards etc. Aft on starboard is a separate, twin bunked cabin with all cupboards, wardrobes etc. Opposite on port is the WC compartment with shower and washbasin. Aft into the saloon you have 2 L-shaped settees, one to port and one to starboard which can be joined to make one large dining area. Aft on the starboard side is a fully equipped galley and opposite on the port side is the chart table. Entrance to the large engine room is by a ¾ height door. A passage on the port side leads aft to the owner's state room where there is an L-shaped settee to starboard and a double berth to port. There is an en-suite WC with all facilities. There are numerous cupboards and ample wardrobe space.

Photo from D.B.L. Imaging.

Moody 52

LOA:	51'9"
LWL:	39'0"
Beam:	14'2"
Draft:	6'9"
Draft:	(deep) 7'5"
Thames meas.:	32 tons
Sail area:	1123 sq.ft.
Engine:	Perkins 6.354 96 HP diesel
Designed by:	Laurent Giles & Partners Ltd
Moulded by:	Halmatic Ltd
Fitted out and marketed by:	A.H. Moody & Son Ltd
Build duration:	1976-1983
Number built:	7

The Moody 52 is another classic design from the drawing board of Laurent Giles & Partners Ltd. She was following on in the Moody tradition as being a true cruising yacht with distinction. She was ketch rigged and suitable for short handed sailing. There were two steering positions, one in a separate aft cockpit and the other in the forward end of the deck saloon for those who did not wish to brave the weather. Her hull was of a fin and skeg configuration. She had a distinctive, stylish deck saloon with good sized side deck and flush foredeck. Her decks were teak laid over GRP. Her internal finish was mainly teak and teak veneer. One of these yachts was built with twin engines for even greater manoeuvrability under power. Her water capacity was 300 gallons and fuel capacity was 300 gallons.

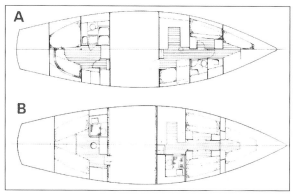

Accommodation: To sleep 8/9 people in 5 cabins including the saloon. As this craft was semi-customized there were alternative layouts offered within the confines of the structural bulkheads. Two alternative layouts illustrated.

Photo from D.B.L. Imaging.

Moody 47/471 & Culverneer 500

LOA:	(47/471): 46'6"
(Culverneer)	
LOA:	49'7"
LWL:	38'9"
Beam:	14'8"
Draft:	(fin) 6'9"
Centreplate:	
	down 9'6" up 4'9"

Displacement:	27,500 lbs
Sail area:	1125 sq.ft.
Engine:	Thorneycroft T140 60HP or T150 66 HP diesel
Designed by:	Bill Dixon
Fitted out, moulded and marketed by:	A.H. Moody & Son Ltd.
Build duration:	1982-1989
Number built:	31

The Moody 47 and her variations was one of the most successful single designs to be built at Swanwick. She underwent a number of design detail changes and re-branding during her production. The final brand was to be the Marksman 47 and 50 (build duration 1988 - 1991); based on the same hull with different deck and superstructure and with a transom extension. All in all a successful design spanning some 9 years in total.

Accommodation: To sleep 6 in 3 cabins excluding saloon. Alternative accommodation layouts were available within the confines of the structural bulkheads. One alternative was:

From forward, chain locker, large WC compartment. Aft with one twin berth cabin to port and one to starboard. Both with access to forward WC. Aft into main saloon with large U-shaped dinette to starboard and shaped settee to port. Chart space aft on port with galley opposite on starboard. Passageway on starboard to main owner's stateroom with central double berth and small settee to starboard. Access to large en suite WC with separate shower compartment. This WC can also be accessed from the chart area. Centre cockpit sloop rigged and wheel steering. Deck storage.

Marksman. Photo by Patrick Roach.

Moody & Marine Projects

1973-2005

This selection of Moody yachts were those jointly developed by Moody and Marine Projects. There were 39 different models totalling some 4233 boats ranging from 27ft to 64ft in length.

Moody 33

LOA:	33'
LWL:	28'5"
Beam:	11'5"
Draft:	5'5"
Displacement:	4.69 tons
Sail Area approx.:	580 sq.ft.
Accommodation:	to sleep 6
Water capacity:	40 gals approx.
Fuel capacity:	40 approx.

Photo from D.B.L. Imaging.

Once the decision had been made for the two companies to cooperate and form a joint venture, work moved on at a pace. Angus Primrose was chosen as the designer and the 33 footer he had designed was the boat selected. In 1972 development work had begun and targets had been set for the first boat to be shown at the Southampton Boat Show in September 1973.

This was achieved and the first boat was shown in the Ocean Hall Marquee in Mayflower Park, Southampton. The first few boats were placed on the market at a few pounds under £10.000 and needless to say, she was an instant success story, with over 242 boats being built, between 1973 and 1978. To all intents and purposes, she was the MkI although this was not her official name. Three other versions, based on the same hull were introduced later - the Moody 33 MkII; Moody 33S and the 333. The total number built from this hull were 494 boats. Over the period of production, there was continuous development and improvement as more modern materials became available - e.g. steering pedestals, replacing wooden toe rails with aluminium etc. It is recalled that the first few boats were also fitted with the Perkins 4.107/8 diesel engine and due to a strike at Perkins, this had to be changed to a Thorneycroft to maintain production levels.

Some of the outstanding features that stayed with the 33 was the sunken anchor well forward, the large centre cockpit and her manoeuvrability under power both ahead and astern. Her high freeboard was well disguised by the flare and the knuckle forward and a certain amount of tumblehome amidships. She had a reverse counter. She was of light displacement and surprisingly responsive and sail needed to be reduced to gain full potential of performance as the wind increased. Her accommodation was spacious with 2 V berths forward, a roomy WC compartment stretching right across the boat with shower, washbasin etc, a saloon with U shaped dinette arrangement to starboard and galley and chart space with quarter berth under, opposite on port. Aft into the large centre cockpit with very large storage locker on starboard. Down into aft cabin with 2 single berths, one to port and one to starboard with central dressing table. Passageway between main cabin and aft cabin was not available until the introduction of the Moody 333.

Photo from D.B.L. Imaging.

Moody 33 Mk II

The Moody 33 MkII was introduced to coincide with the Southampton Boat Show, September 1978 and continued in production until June 1981 with 121 boats of this type being built. Angus had reworked the deck and superstructure which appeared more angular and seemed to give even more space below decks. The main change below was to the saloon with a staggered forward bulkhead putting the WC to starboard and a settee to port and starboard, a centrally mounted table and galley to port with chart table opposite to starboard. The aft cabin was accessed from the cockpit.

Moody 333

This was to be the last centre cockpit to be based on this hull. She was introduced in September 1981 again to coincide with the Southampton Boat Show and finished in 1983, having built 77 of this version. At this time a passageway from the main saloon to the aft cabin had been incorporated. The aft cabin had a double berth and dressing table. The deck geometry had

Photo from David Moody collection.

been changed to give her a sleeker look. There were changes to the saloon layout but maintaining the central dining table, a galley to port and chart space.

Photo from D.B.L. Imaging.

Moody 33S

This was an aft cockpit version using the same 33 hull introduced in September 1979 again to coincide with the Southampton Boat Show. This model ceased production in February 1982, with 54 boats having been built. She had generous accommodation to sleep 6 with 2 berths forward, separate WC, U shaped dinette to starboard with table, settee berth to port with galley aft. Opposite chart space and double enclosed quarter berth. Engine option a 2 cyl Buhk or Thorneycroft T90 diesel. Water capacity 40 gals. Fuel capacity 35 gals. Good sized aft cockpit with wheel steering.

Moody 30

LOA: 30'0" • *LWL:* 26'0" • *Beam:* 10'1"
• *Draft:* 4'9" • *Displacement:* 8100 lbs
• *Working Sail area:* 373 sq.ft. • *Engine:*
Volvo Penta MD 11C 23 HP Diesel
• *Build duration:* September 1975 -
November 1979 • *Number built:* 162

Accommodation: to sleep 6 in 2 cabins
including saloon.

Aft cockpit with tiller or wheel steering.

Moody 36

LOA: 36'0" • *LWL:* 30'0" • *Beam:* 12'4"
• *Draft:* 5'0" • *Displacement:* 14,700 lbs
• *Working Sail area:* 506 sq.ft. • *Engine:*
Thorneycroft T90 35 HP diesel • *Build
duration:* December 1977 - August 1981
• *Number built:* 89

Accommodation to sleep 6 in 3 cabins
including saloon. Passageway to aft
cabin.

Centre cockpit with wheel steering.

Moody 39

LOA: 38' 6" • *LWL:* 32'6" • *Beam:* 13'4"
• *Draft:* 5'6" • *Displacement:* 18,150 lbs
• *Working Sail area:* 595 sq.ft. • *Engine:*
Thorneycroft T108 47 HP diesel • *Build
duration:* 1975 - 1978 • *Number built:* 82

Accommodation: to sleep 8 in 4 cabins
including saloon. Passageway between
saloon and aft cabin. Centre cockpit with
wheel steering.

Moody 40

LOA: 39'6" • *LWL:* 32'6" • *Beam:* 13'4"
• *Draft:* 5'6" • *Displacement:* 18,150 lbs
• *Working Sail area:* 595 sq.ft. • *Engine:*
Thorneycroft T108 46 HP diesel • *Build
duration:* 1978-1981 • *Number built:* 56

Accommodation to sleep 6 excluding
saloon. Passageway to aft cabin.

Centre cockpit with wheel steering.

Photos from D.B.L. Imaging.

Moody 29

LOA: 29'8" • *LWL:* 25'0" • *Beam:* 10'6" • *Draft:* 4'6" • *Draft:* bilge 3'6" • *Displacement:* 7300 lbs • *Working Sail area:* 367 sq.ft. • *Engine:* Bukh DV20ME 20 HP diesel • *Build duration:* July 1980 - July 1983 • *Number built:* 145

Accommodation: to sleep 6 in 2 cabins inc saloon.

Aft cockpit with tiller steering.

Moody 36 DS

LOA: 36'0" • *LWL:* 30'0" • *Beam:* 12'4" • *Draft:* 5'0" • *Displacement:* 14,700 lbs • *Working Sail area:* 506 sq.ft. • *Engine:* Thorneycroft T90 35 HP diesel • *Build duration:* September 1980 - June 1981 • *Number built:* 4

Accommodation: to sleep 6 inc the deck saloon.

Aft cockpit with wheel steering.

Moody 36S

LOA: 36'0" • *LWL:* 30'0" • *Beam:* 12'4" • *Draft:* 5'0" • *Displacement:* 14,700 lbs • *Working Sail area:* 506 sq.ft. • *Engine:* Thorneycroft T90 35 HP diesel • *Build duration:* September 1981 - March 1983 • *Number built:* 19

Accommodation: to sleep 6 inc saloon.

Aft cockpit with wheel steering.

Moody 41/419

Photo is of the 419.

LOA: (41). / 41'0" • *LWL:* 34'0" • *Beam:* 13'2" • *Draft:* 6'0" • *LOA:* (419) 41'9" • *Displacement:* 20,600 lbs • *Working Sail area:* 724 sq.ft. • *Engine:* Thorneycroft T108 48 HP diesel • *Build duration:* (41): December 1981 - August 1984 • (419) August 1984 - July 1986 • *Number built:* 41-53 built, 419-60 built

Accommodation: to sleep 6/7 in 4 cabins including saloon.

Centre cockpit with wheel steering.

Moody 27

LOA: 27'8" • *LWL:* 21'11" • *Beam:* 9'8" • *Draft:* (fin) 4'8" (bilge) 3'5" • *Displacement:* 5750 lbs • *Working sail area including genoa:* 412 sq.ft. • *Engine:* Volvo Penta MD 7B 17 HP diesel or Volvo 2002 18 HP diesel • *Build duration:* December 1981 - August 1985 • *Number built:* 162

Accommodation: to sleep 5/6 including saloon.

Aft cockpit tiller steering.

Moody 34/346 *(Moody 34 below)*

LOA: (34) 33'5" • *LOA:* (346) 34'5" • *LWL:* 27'9" • *Beam:* 11'8" *Displacement:* 11,200 lbs • *Working Sail area:* 514 sq.ft • *Engine:* Thorneycroft T80/T90 35 HP diesel or Volvo 2003 28HP diesel • *Build duration:* (34) June 1983 - June 1986, (346) June 1986 - July 1990 • *Number built:* (34) 165 (346) 254

Accommodation: to sleep 6 in 3 cabins inc. saloon. Moody 346 incorporated a sugar scoop transom.

Moody 31 (Mk I & II) *(Mk I below)*

LOA: 30.75' • *LWL:* 25.42' • *Beam:* 10.5' • *Draft:* (fin) 5' (bilge) 3.67' • *Displacement:* 9966 lbs • *Working Sail area:* 503 sq.ft. • *Engine:* Volvo 2003 28HP diesel • *Build duration:* (Mk I & II) September 1983 - June 1991 • *Number built:* (combined) 305

Accommodation: to sleep 6 in 3 cabins inc saloon. Aft cockpit with tiller or wheel steering. Mk II incorporated sugar scoop transom.

Moody 37/376 *(Moody 37 below)*

LOA: (37) 37' • *LOA:* (376) 37'10"

• *LWL:* 31'3" • *Beam:* 12'6" • *Draft:* (fin) 5'6" (Scheel) 4'6" • *Displacement:* 16, 250 lbs • *Working sail area:* 639 sq.ft • *Standard Engine:* Thorneycroft T90 35 HP diesel • *Build duration:* July 1985 - August 1991 • *Number built:* 313

Accommodation: to sleep 7 in 3 cabins inc saloon and passageway. Centre cockpit with wheel steering. Moody 376 incorporated sugar scoop transom.

Photos by Tony Willey.

Moody 28

LOA: 27'6" • *LWL:* 23'4" • *Beam:* 10'0" • *Draft:* (fin) 5'0" (bilge) 3'6" • *Displacement:* (fin) 6550 lbs (bilge) 6850 lbs • *Sail area:* 355 sq.ft. • *Engine:* Volvo Penta 2002 18 HP diesel • *Build duration:* December 1985 - June 1987 • *Number built:* 70

Accommodation: to sleep 6 in 3 cabins inc saloon.

Aft cockpit with tiller steering.

Moody 422/425 *(Moody 425 below)*

LOA: 42' • *LWL:* 34.25 ft. • *Beam:* 13.34 ft. • *Draft:* (fin) 6' (shoal) 4.66' • *Displacement:* 21,780 lbs • *Sail area:* 781 sq.ft. • *Engine:* Thorneycroft 50 HP diesel • *Build duration:* 422 September 86 - June 88 • 425 August 1988 - July 1991 • *Number built:* (422) - 72 (425) - 116

Accommodation: to sleep 8 in 4 cabins inc saloon and passageway.

Centre cockpit with wheel steering.

Moody Eclipse 33

LOA: 32'6" • *LWL:* 28' • *Beam:* 11'2" • *Draft:* (fin) 4'9" • *Draft:* (bilge) 3'8" • *Displacement:* (fin) 12,465 lbs (bilge) 13,000 lbs • *Sail area:* 525 sq.ft. • *Engine:* Volvo 2003 28 HP or Turbo version 43 HP or Perkins Perama M30 29HP diesel • *Build duration:* December 1987 - April 1994 • *Number built:* 253

Accommodation: to sleep 6 in 3 cabins inc saloon.

Aft cockpit with deck saloon and wheel steering.

Moody 336

LOA: 33'6" • *LWL:* 28'9" • *Beam:* 11'7" • *Draft:* (fin) 5'6" (bilge) 3'11" • *Displacement:* 12,584 lbs • *Working sail area:* 478 sq.ft. • *Engine:* Volvo 2003 28HP or Perkins Perama M30 29HP diesel • *Build duration:* December 1988 - June 1996 • *Number built:* 200

Accommodation: to sleep 6 in 3 cabins including saloon. Aft cockpit with wheel steering.

146

Moody Eclipse 43

LOA: 42.5' • *LWL:* 36.8' • *Beam:* 14' • *Draft:* 4.83' • *Displacement:* 23,000 lbs • *Engine:* Perkins M80T 78HP diesel • *Build duration:* December 1989 - August 1991 • *Number built:* 38

Accommodation: to sleep 8 in 4 cabins inc saloon.

In mast furling and furling headsail.

Aft cockpit with deck saloon and wheel steering.

Moody Eclipse 38

LOA: 37'6" • *LWL:* 32'3" • *Beam:* 13" • *Draft:* 4'6" • *Displacement:* 16250 lbs • *Sail area:* 777 sq.ft. in mast furling and furling genoa • *Engine:* Perkins M60 59HP diesel • *Build duration:* December 1990 - February 1992 • *Number built:* 24

Accommodation: to sleep 6 in 3 cabins inc saloon.

Aft cockpit with deck saloon and wheel steering.

Moody 35

LOA: 34'6" • *LWL:* 28'10" • *Beam:* 11'11" • *Draft:* (fin) 5'3" (bilge) 3'11" • *Displacement:* (fin) 12,800 lbs (bilge) 13,300 lbs • *Working Sail area:* 505 sq.ft • *Engine:* Thorneycroft T80 35 HP, Perkins Perama 34 HP or Volvo 2040 39 HP diesel • *Build duration:* July 1990 - April 1996 • *Number built:* 192

Accommodation: to sleep 6 in 3 cabins inc saloon.

Centre cockpit with wheel steering.

Moody 44

LOA: 44' • *LWL:* 36' • *Beam:* 13'8" • *Draft:* (fin) 6'6"(shoal) 4'11" • *Displacement:* (fin) 23,000 lbs (shoal) 23,631 lbs • *Sail area:* 994 sq.ft. in mast furling and furling genoa • *Engine:* Perkins M50 or Volvo MD 22L 50 HP diesel • *Build duration:* August 1991 - September 1996 • *Number built:* 114

Accommodation: to sleep 8 in 4 cabins inc saloon.

Centre cockpit with wheel steering.

Moody 38

LOA: 37'6" ● *LWL:* 31'6" ● *Beam:* 12'8" ● *Draft:* (fin) 5'9" (shoal) 4'6" ● *Displacement:* 18,000 lbs ● *Sail area:* 740 sq.ft. in mast furling and furling genoa ● *Engine:* Perkins M35 34HP, Perkins M50 50HP or Volvo MD22L 50HP ● *Build duration:* September 91 - November 1996 ● *Number built:* 163

Accommodation: to sleep 7 in 4 cabins inc saloon and passageway.

Centre cockpit wheel steering.

Moody S31

LOA: 31'9" ● *LWL:* 26'6" ● *Beam:* 10'10" ● *Draft:* (fin) 5'6" (bilge) 3'9" ● *Displacement:* (fin) 10,218 lbs (bilge) 10617 lbs ● *Sail area:* (mast head) 385 sq.ft. ● *Engine:* Volvo MD2020 19HP diesel sail drive ● *Build duration:* June 1994 - February 1998 ● *Number built:* 145

Accommodation: to sleep 6 in 3 cabins inc. saloon.

Aft cockpit with tiller or wheel steering.

Moody S38

LOA: 39' ● *LWL:* 32'6" ● *Beam:* 12'11" ● *Draft:* (fin) 6'3" (shoal) 4'11" ● *Displacement:* 19,064 lbs ● *Sail area:* 798 sq.ft. ● *Engine:* Volvo MD 2040 40HP diesel ● *Build duration:* September 10995 - June 1998 ● *Number built:* 60

Accommodation: to sleep 6 /8 in 3/4 cabins inc saloon.

Aft cockpit wheel steering.

Moody 36

LOA: 36'9" ● *LWL:* 30'4" ● *Beam:* 12'3" ● *Draft:* (fin) 5'9" (bilge) 3'11" ● *Displacement:* (fin) 17996 lbs (bilge) 18,543 lbs ● *Engine:* Volvo MD2040 40 HP diesel ● *Working Sail area:* 489 sq.ft. ● *Build duration:* July 1996 - October 2000 ● *Number built:* 118

Accommodation: to sleep 7 in 4 cabins inc saloon and passageway.

Centre cockpit wheel steering.

Photos by Tony Willey (Moody S31 & 36), Norman Burniston (Moody 38) and Tom Benn (Moody S38).

Moody 40

LOA: 40'2" • *LWL:* 33'8" • *Beam:* 13'3" • *Draft:* (fin) 6'1", (shoal) 4'11" • *Displacement:* (fin) 23,100 lbs, (shoal) 23,597 lbs in mast furling, furling genoa • *Sail area:* 828 sq.ft. • *Build duration:* December 96 - December 98 • *Number built:* 4 • *Engine:* Volvo Penta MD 22L 50HP diesel engine.

Accommodation: to sleep 7/8 in 4 cabins including the saloon and passageway. She had a centre cockpit with wheel steering. There were a small number of early Moody 40s with a different positioned aft WC.

Moody 42 *(above)*

LOA: 42'2" • *LWL:* 34'10" • *Beam:* 13'3" • *Draft:* (fin) 6'1", (shoal) 4'11" • *Displacement:* (fin) 23,144 lbs, (shoal) 23,641 lbs in mast furling, furling genoa • *Sail area:* 828 sq.ft. • *Build duration:* August 99 - March 02 • *Number built:* 55 • *Engine:* Volvo Penta MD 22L 50HP diesel engine.

Accommodation: to sleep 7/8 in 4 cabins including the saloon and passageway. She had a centre cockpit with wheel steering. There were a small number of early Moody 40s with a different positioned aft WC.

Moody 46

LOA: 46'2" • *LWL:* 39'4" • *Beam:* 14'5" • *Draft:* (fin) 6'9" (shoal) 5'3" • *Displacement:* (fin) 31,878 lbs (shoal) 32,714 lbs • *Sail area:* Total furling system. Cutter rig 1216 sq.ft. • *Engine:* Volvo TMD 22 78 HP or Yanmar 4JH2 THE 75 HP diesel • *Build duration:* December 1997 - June 2001 • *Number built:* 55

Accommodation: to sleep 7 in 4 cabins exc. saloon. Raised saloon, centre cockpit wheel steering. Lowering transom bathing platform.

Moody 47

LOA: 478" • *LWL:* 39'5" • *Beam:* 14'5" • *Draft:* (fin) 6'9" (shoal) 5'3" • *Displacement:* (fin) 32,890 lbs (shoal) 33,726 lbs • *Sail area:* Total furling system. Cutter rig 1216 sq. • *Engine:* Yanmar 4JH3 78 HP diesel • *Build duration:* August 2001 - October 2004 • *Number built:* 46

Accommodation: to sleep 7 in 4 cabins exc. saloon. Raised saloon, centre cockpit wheel steering. Lowering transom bathing platform.

Photos by Tony Willey (Moody 42 & 46) and Tom Benn (Moody 47).

Moody 54

LOA: 54'11" • *LWL:* 46'1" • *Beam:* 15'11" • *Draft:* (fin) 7'6" (shoal) 5'11" • *Displacement:* 44,132 lbs • *Sail area:* Total furling system cutter rig 1693 sq.ft. • *Engine:* Yanmar 4JH2 - UT (B) E100HP diesel • *Build duration:* December 1999 - March 2004 • *Number built:* 55

Accommodation: to sleep 7 in 4 cabins exc. saloon.

Raised saloon centre cockpit wheel steering. Lowering transom bathing platform.

Moody 64

LOA: 63'5" • *LWL:* 54'3" • *Beam:* 17'6" • *Draft:* (fin) 8'6" (shoal) 6'6" • *Displacement:* Light 63360 lbs Full 69080 lbs • *Sail area:* 1794 sq.ft. Total furling system cutter rig • *Engine:* Yanmar 4LHA - STE 230 HP diesel • *Build duration:* March 2002 - October 2004 • *Number built:* 14

Accommodation: to sleep 8 in 5 cabins inc passageway, excluding saloon.

Raised saloon centre cockpit. Twin wheel steering. Lowering transom bathing platform.

Moody 38

LOA: 38'6" • *LWL:* 32'1" • *Beam:* 12'4" • *Draft:* (fin) 6'3" (shoal) 4'9" • *Displacement:* (fin) 18266 lbs (shoal) 18352 lbs • *Sail area:* 662 sq.ft. • *Engine:* Yanmar 4JH3 56HP diesel • *Build duration:* January 2000 - February 2003 • *Number built:* 37

Accommodation: to sleep 6 in 3 cabins inc saloon. Centre cockpit with wheel steering.

Moody 56

LOA: 56'11" • *LWL:* 46'2" • *Beam:* 15'11" • *Draft:* (fin) 7'6" (shoal) 5'11" • *Displacement:* 44,132 lbs • *Sail area:* Total furling system cutter rig 1693 sq.ft. • *Engine:* Yanmar 4JH2 - UT(B)E 100 HP diesel • *Build duration:* January 2004 - June 2005 • *Number built:* 3

Accommodation: to sleep 7 in 4 cabin exc. saloon. Raised saloon centre cockpit wheel steering. Lowering transom bathing platform.

Photos by Tony Willey (Moody 54 & 56) and Tom Benn (Moody 38).

Moody Excel Range

The ever increasing pressure on companies to remain competitive, meant that larger boats were the only way forward. Therefore, the smaller boat which could be said to be the starter end of the market was being neglected. Moody considered this situation very seriously and attempted to re-brand and re-introduce the Moody S31 to the market, and to continue to develop a 34 foot Bill Dixon design. The development of this boat had already begun with Marine Projects when it was decided that the product would probably not be viable. Therefore it was shelved. With these two models available and there still being potential in the market for this type of craft, we decided to go out and find a new manufacturer. We eventually chose Prout Catamarans to produce these boats. They were to be called the Moody Excel 31 and Excel 34 and again, both were Bill Dixon designs. Despite their best efforts, this project had only limited success and the range barely lasted two years.

There were 5 Excel 31s produced for a charter company and one for a private individual, but again, unfortunately, even though they had learnt how to build these boats economically, they could not compete with the products now coming in from France and Germany so after this initial run, it was decided to discontinue. The 34 also ran for two years. Four of this model were produced. Everything was done to keep the cost to a minimum even to the extent of fitting a sail drive to the engine. She was a very roomy centre cockpit design with wheel steering. She also met the same fate as the 31.

Moody Excel 31

LOA: 31'9" • *LWL:* 26'6" • *Beam:* 10'10" • *Draft:* (fin) 5'6" (bilge) 3'9" • *Displacement:* (fin) 10218 lbs (bilge) 10617 lbs • *Working Sail area:* 412 sq.ft • *Engine:* Volvo MD2020 19 HP diesel with sail drive • *Build duration:* 1999 - 2001

Accommodation: to sleep 6 in 3 cabins including saloon.

Aft cockpit with tiller or wheel steering.

Moody Excel 34

LOA: 34' • *LWL:* 29.20' • *Beam:* 11.51' • *Draft:* (fin) 5.58' (bilge) 3.87' • *Displacement:* light (fin) 12,786 lbs (bilge) 13,331 lbs • *Working Sail area:* 503 sq.ft. • *Engine:* Volvo MD2030 29 HP diesel sail drive • *Build duration:* 1999 - 2001

Accommodation: to sleep 6 in 3 cabins including saloon. Passageway between saloon and aft cabin.

Centre cockpit with wheel steering.

Moody and VT Halmatic Ltd

A new cooperation was formed between Moody and VT Halmatic Ltd. in late 2003/2004 to build the Moody product. We had worked with Halmatic in the past on various projects in the 70s and 80s therefore we were quite comfortable with this arrangement. The first boat to be jointly developed was a 49 foot Bill Dixon design. Halmatic developed and produced this boat in under 12 months which was a great achievement. Halmatic also re-developed the Moody 64 into a 66ft and took over the manufacturing of the 56. We now had a 3 boat range which was receiving good interest internationally. This cooperation was in its early stages when Moody was sold at the end of 2005. In the short time we were involved with Halmatic, they proved themselves to be committed and a very good choice of manufacturer who took great pride in the product.

Moody 49

LOA: 48'7" • *LWL:* 40'7" • *Beam:* 14'5" • *Draft:* (fin) 6'7" (shoal) 5'3" • *Displacement:* (fin) 34, 556 lbs • *Sail area:* Total furling system cutter rig 1347 sq.ft. • *Engine:* Yanmar 4JH3 - HTE 100HP diesel • *Build duration:* 2004 - 2005 • *Number built:* 5 by the end of 2005

Accommodation: to sleep 7 in 4 cabins inc passageway, exc. saloon. Raised saloon, centre cockpit wheel steering Lowering transom bathing platform

Moody 56

LOA: 56'11" • *LWL:* 46'2" • *Beam:* 15'11" • *Draft:* (fin) 7'6" (shoal) 5'11" • *Displacement:* 44,132 lbs • *Sail area:* Total furling system cutter rig 1693 sq.ft. • *Engine:* Yanmar 4JH2 - UT (B) E 100HP diesel • *Build duration:* 2005 • *Number built:* 0, by end of 2005

Accommodation to sleep 7 in 4 cabins inc passageway exc. saloon. Raised saloon, centre cockpit, wheel steering lowering transom bathing platform.

Moody 66

LOA: 65'9" • *LWL:* 54'3" • *Beam:* 17'6" • *Draft:* (fin) 8'6" (shoal) 6'6" • *Displacement:* (light) 63360 lbs (heavy) 69080 lbs • *Sail area:* Total furling system cutter rig 1794 sq.ft. • *Engine:* Yanmar 4LHA - STE 230 HP diesel • *Build duration:* 2005 • *Number built:* 1 by end of 2005

Accommodation to sleep 8 in 5 cabins inc passageway, exc. saloon. Raised saloon centre cockpit twin wheel steering. Lowering transom bathing platform.

Photos by Tony Willey (Moody 66) and John Banford (Moody 49 & 56).

How the transom changed over the years

circa. 1973-1985

circa. 1985-1991

circa. 1990-1994

circa. 1991-1996

circa. 1987-1992

circa. 1997-2005

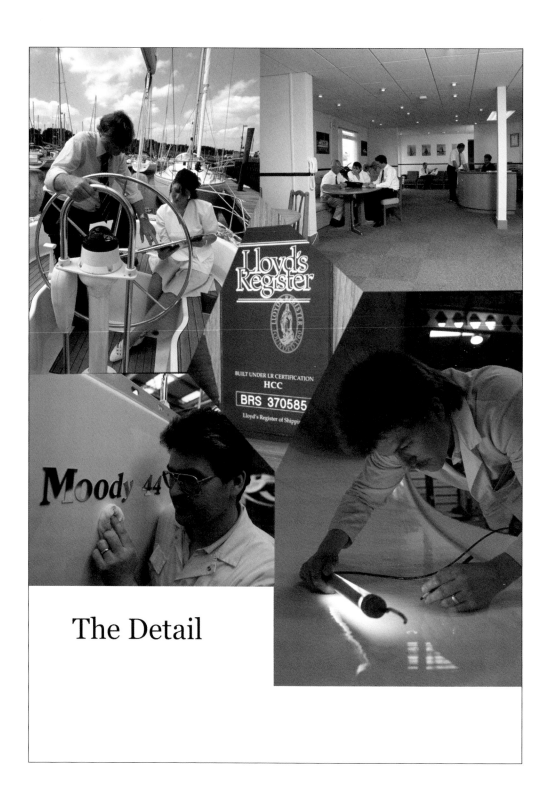

The Detail

Photos by Tony Willey.

Explaining the List

The following list has been prepared where possible in chronological order and has been gathered from a variety of sources. It catalogues the majority of craft that were manufactured at Swanwick and Warsash from 1935. It also lists the numbers of boats bearing the Moody name that were built by other manufacturers. There have been a number of collaborations to build the Moody product, such as Marine Projects, VT Halmatic Ltd. and Prout Catamarans.

 The private yacht information has been mainly researched through the Lloyds Register of Yachts 1935 through to 1980 and from information out of my own personal archive. The Admiralty craft information has been researched and provided by Philip Simons and Terry Holtham, (Coastal Forces Historians). Admiralty numbering was generally made up of the first two digits being the year of order and the last 3/4 digits were the numbers given to the vessel. For example, 37290 would mean ordered 1937 and 290 was the identification number. Where possible, all information available has been included in the list. Any blanks mean that the information was not available as far as I know!

Glossary

HDML	Harbour Defence Motor Launch	L	Lost
MSB	Motor Survey Boat	S	Sold
FMB	Fast Motor Boat	T	Transferred
MPP	Motor Pulling Pinnace	B	BTB (Bought To Produce) Scrapped
HL	Harbour Launch	R	Returned
MC	Motor Cutter	P	Pulling boat - Register
NST	Naval Storing Tender	WOC	Written Off Charge
LCA	Landing Craft Assault	C	Cancelled
MFV	Motor Fishing Vessel	HO	Handed Over
LOA	Length Over All	BTP	Scrapped
LWL	Length Water Line	FS	For Sale
Draft	From Waterline to under side of keel	FD	For Disposal
Aux Berm	Auxiliary Bermudan	DE	Devonport
Aux Sloop	Auxiliary Sloop		
LBS	London Boat Show		
Cyl	Cylinder		
BHP	Brake Horse Power		
GRP	Glass Reinforced Plastic		
CC	Centre Cockpit		
AC	Aft Cockpit		

Private yachts built by Moody at Swanwick from 1935

Yacht name	Yard	Owner	Designer	Place of build	Year	Type	Engine	LOA ft	LWL ft	Beam ft	Draft ft	Sail area (sq.ft)	Tons	Build Material	Photo
Vindilis		T. Harrison Butler	T. Harrison Butler MD	Swanwick	1935	Aux Berm Yawl	2cyl Stuart Turner Petrol	30	22.5	8.7	4.4	410	7	wood	yes
Delight		T.W.Holland	F.Shepherd	Swanwick	1935	Aux ketch	4 cyl Morris Paraffin	32	26	9	5	580	9	wood	yes
Eila		S. Bourne	F.Shepherd	Swanwick	1935	Aux Berm cutter	4 cyl. Morris Petrol	35.7	26.5	9	5	559	9	wood	yes
Zingara		Dr Cargill	T Harrison Butler MD	Swanwick	1936	Aux Berm cutter	8bhp Handy Billy Thornycroft Petrol	29'6"	25	8.5	5	460	7	wood	yes
Andrillot (Vertue Class)		R.A Kinnersley	Laurent Giles & Partners Ltd	Swanwick	1936	Cutter Sail no.1		25.2	21	7.1	4.5	370	5	wood	yes
Lindy II		R.T.Pemberton	T.Harrison Butler MD	Swanwick	1936	Aux.Berm Yawl	2 cyl. Stuart Turner Petrol	30	22.5	8.7	4.4	410	7	wood	yes
Mystery		F.P. Usborn	Robert Clark	Swanwick	1936	Aux Berm Cutter	4 cyl Gray Petrol	39	26.2	8.7	5.5	598	10	wood	yes
Edith Rose		R.S.L. Crossley	T. Harrison Butler MD	Swanwick	1937	Aux Berm Cutter	4 cyl Brooke Petrol	29.5	23	8.6	6	417	7	wood	yes
Fubbs		V.N. Peel	F. Shepherd	Swanwick	1937	Aux Berm Cutter	4 cyl. Parsons Petrol	37.4	27.5	9.4	5.5	573	11	wood	yes
Norana		B. W. Clay	Bernard W. Clay	Swanwick	1937	Single screw Motor yacht	6 cylinder Gardiner Diesel	60	56	14.7	5.2		48	wood	
Silver Streak		H.R.Watt	F. Shepherd	Swanwick	1937	Aux Berm ketch	3 cyl Ailsa Craig Diesel	44.5	31.8	10.2	6	775	15	wood	yes
Zest Teal class		Miss A.H. Clay	A.R.Luke	Swanwick	1937	Berm Sloop		30.5	20.3	7	5	401	5	wood	
Kayak (Channel Class)		D.D.Capper	Laurent Giles & Partners Ltd	Swanwick	1938	Aux. Berm Cutter	4 cyl Gray petrol	37.8	26.2	8.7	6	750	10	wood	yes
Triune of Troy (Channel class)		Lord Russell of Liverpool	Laurent Giles & Partners Ltd	Swanwick	1938	Aux Berm Cutter	4 cyl Gray petrol	37.9	26	8.8	6	600	10	wood	yes
Lady Christabel		Sir Maurice Jenks	F.Shepherd	Swanwick	1938	Twin screw motor yacht	2X 4cyl Morris petrol	38.2	35.2	9.8	3		14	wood	yes
Amokura		Maj. E.S.Harston	F.Shepherd	Swanwick	1939	Aux Berm Yawl	4 cyl Gray Petrol	50.3	37.6	12	7	1020	24	wood	yes
Josephine II		Cosby Smallpiece	K.H.Reimers	Swanwick	1939	Berm Sloop		32	25.4	7.5	5	323	7	wood	yes

Admiralty small craft built by Moody 1940 to 1947

Type	No	Owner	Designer	Place of build	Year	Order date	Engine	LOA	LWL	Beam	Draft	Tons	Material	Photo
HDML	1067	Admiralty	Admiralty	Swanwick	8.5.41	31.7.40	2 x 300 bhp Gardner Diesels	72	69	15	4.5 / 5.5	54	wood	
HDML	1068	Admiralty	Admiralty	Swanwick	25.6.41	31.7.40	2 x 300 bhp Gardner diesels	72	69	15	4.5 / 5.5	54	wood	
HDML	1148	Admiralty	Admiralty	Swanwick	23.4.42	30.5.41	2 x 300bhp Gardner diesels	72	69	15	4.5 /5.5	54	wood	
HDML	1149	Admiralty	Admiralty	Swanwick	29.5.42	30.5.41	2 x 300bhp Gardner diesels	72	69	15	4.5/5.5	54	wood	
HDML	1221	Admiralty	Admiralty	Swanwick	6.8.42	17.12.41	2x300 bhp Gardner diesels	72	69	15	4.5/5.5	54	wood	Yes
HDML	1222	Admiralty	Admiralty	Swanwick	9.3.43	17.12.41	2x300 bhp Gardner diesels	72	69	15	4.5/5.5	54	wood	
HDML	1276	Admiralty	Admiralty	Swanwick	21.1.43	24.4.42	2x300 bhp Gardner diesels	72	69	15	4.5/5.5	54	wood	
HDML	1277	Admiralty	Admiralty	Swanwick	20.3.43	24.4.42	2x300 bhp Gardner diesels	72	69	15	4.5/5.5	54	wood	
HDML	1278	Admiralty	Admiralty	Swanwick	20.5.43	24.4.42	2x300 bhp Gardner diesels	72	69	15	4.5/5.5	54	wood	
HDML	1374	Admiralty	Admiralty	Swanwick	31.7.43	11.9.42	2x300 bhp Gardner diesels	72	69	15	4.5/5.5	54	wood	
HDML	1375	Admiralty	Admiralty	Swanwick	2.10.43	11.9.42	2x300 bhp Gardner diesels	72	69	15	4.5/5.5	54	wood	
HDML	1421	Admiralty	Admiralty	Swanwick	23.12.43	19.3.43	2x300 bhp Gardner diesels	72	69	15	4.5/5.5	54	wood	
HDML	1422	Admiralty	Admiralty	Swanwick	3.3.44	19.3.43	2x300 bhp Gardner diesels	72	69	15	4.5/5.5	54	wood	
HDML	1423	Admiralty	Admiralty	Swanwick	0.4.44	19.3.43	2x300 bhp Gardner diesels	72	69	15	4.5/5.5	54	wood	
HDML	1488	Admiralty	Admiralty	Swanwick	11.11.44	29.1.44	2x300 bhp Gardner diesels	72	69	15	4.5/5.5	54	wood	
HDML	1489	Admiralty	Admiralty	Swanwick	27.1.45	29.1.44	2x300 Gardner diesels	72	69	15	4.5/5.5	54	wood	
MFV	994	Admiralty	Admiralty	subcontracted out		4.12.44	1x60 bhp Chrysler petrol	49.75	45	15.25	3.75/5.75	28.5	wood	
MFV	995	Admiralty	Admiralty	Swanwick	12.45	4.12.44	1x60 bhp Chrysler petrol	49.75	45	15.25	3.75/5.75	28.5	wood	
MSB	37290	Admiralty	Admiralty	Swanwick	1938	31/12/37	Ferry BM petrol	28		7'11"	2'6"	5.1	wood	Yes
MSB	37291	Admiralty	Admiralty	Swanwick	1938	31/12/37	Ferry BM petrol	28		7'11"	2'6"	5.1	wood	
FMB	39507	Admiralty	Admiralty	Swanwick	1940	28/11/39	FerryFordV8 petrol	25		7'	18"	1.9	wood	Yes
FMB	39508	Admiralty	Admiralty	Swanwick	1940	28/11/39	"	25		"	"	"	wood	
FMB	39509	Admiralty	Admiralty	Swanwick	1940	28/11/39	"	25		"	"	"	wood	
FMB	39510	Admiralty	Admiralty	Swanwick	1940	28/11/39	"	25		"	"	"	wood	
FMB	39511	Admiralty	Admiralty	Swanwick	1940	28/11/39	FerryFordV8 petrol	25		7'11"	18"	1.9	wood	
FMB	39512	Admiralty	Admiralty	Swanwick	1940	28/11/39	"	25		"	"	"	wood	
FMB	40168	Admiralty	Admiralty	Swanwick	1941	5/10/40	"	25		"	"	"	wood	
FMB	40169	Admiralty	Admiralty	Swanwick	1941	5/10/40	"	25		"	"	"	wood	
FMB	40170	Admiralty	Admiralty	Swanwick	1941	"	"	25		"	"	"	wood	
FMB	40171	Admiralty	Admiralty	Swanwick	1941	"	"	25		"	"	"	wood	
FMB	40210	Admiralty	Admiralty	Swanwick	1941	29/11/40	VosperMk3 Ford V8 petrol	45		10.6	2'	8	wood	Yes
FMB	40211	Admiralty	Admiralty	Swanwick	1941	"	"	45		10.6	2'	8	wood	
FMB	40212	Admiralty	Admiralty	Swanwick	1941	"	"	45		10.6	2'	8	wood	
MSB	41568	Admiralty	Admiralty	Swanwick	1942	31/7/41	Ferry BM4petrol	25		7'3"	2'2"	3.3	wood	

Type	No	Owner	Designer	Place of build	Year	Order date	Engine	LOA	LWL	Beam	Draft	Tons	Material	Photo
MSB	41569	Admiralty	Admiralty	Swanwick	1942	"	"	25		"	"	"	wood	
MPP	41601	Admiralty	Admiralty	Swanwick	1942	31/7/41	Dorman4DSM Diesel	36		9'9"	1'8"	6	wood	Yes
MPP	41602	Admiralty	Admiralty	Swanwick	1942	"	"	36		"	"	"	wood	
MPP	41603	Admiralty	Admiralty	Swanwick	1942	"	"	36		"	"	"	wood	
MPP	41604	Admiralty	Admiralty	Swanwick	1942	"	"	36		"	"	"	wood	
MPP	41605	Admiralty	Admiralty	Swanwick	1942	"	"	36		"	"	"	wood	
MPP	41606	Admiralty	Admiralty	Swanwick	1942	"	"	36		"	"	"	wood	
MSB	41775	Admiralty	Admiralty	Swanwick	1943	19/12/41	Parsons& Co H4M Petrol	28		7'11"	2'6"	5	wood	
MSB	41776	Admiralty	Admiralty	Swanwick	1943	19/12/41		28		"	"	"	wood	
MSB	41777	Admiralty	Admiralty	Swanwick	1943	19/12/41	FerryBM4 petrol	25		7'3"	2'2"	3.3	wood	Yes
MSB	41778	Admiralty	Admiralty	Swanwick	1943	"	"	25		"	"	"	wood	
MSB	4187	Admiralty	Admiralty	Swanwick	1941	15/10.41	Parsons&Co H4M Petrol	28		7'11"	2'6"	5.1	wood	
MSB	4188	Admiralty	Admiralty	Swanwick	1941	"	"	28		"	"	"	wood	
MSB	4189	Admiralty	Admiralty	Swanwick	1941	"	"	28		"	"	"	wood	
MSB	42354	Admiralty	Admiralty	Swanwick	1943	18/2/42	ParsonsH4M Petrol	25		7'3"	2'2"	3.3	wood	
MSB	42355	Admiralty	Admiralty	Swanwick	1943	"	"	25		"	"	"	wood	
MSB	42356	Admiralty	Admiralty	Swanwick	1943	"	"	25		"	"	"	wood	
MSB	42357	Admiralty	Admiralty	Swanwick	1943	18/2/42	Parsons H4M Petrol	28		7'11"	2'6"	5	wood	
MSB	42358	Admiralty	Admiralty	Swanwick	1943	"	"	28		"	"	"	wood	
HL	42619	Admiralty	Admiralty	Swanwick	1943	8/6/42	KelvinF4 petrol	36		9'9"	1'8"	6	wood	Yes
HL	42620	Admiralty	Admiralty	Swanwick	1943	"	"	36		"	"	"	wood	
HL	42621	Admiralty	Admiralty	Swanwick	1943	"	"	36		"	"	"	wood	
HL	42622	Admiralty	Admiralty	Swanwick	1943	"	"	36		"	"	"	wood	
HL	42623	Admiralty	Admiralty	Swanwick	1943	"	"	36		"	"	"	wood	
HL	42624	Admiralty	Admiralty	Swanwick	1943	20/8/43	"	36		"	"	"	wood	
HL	42821	Admiralty	Admiralty	Swanwick	1943	15/9/42	VosperV8Ford Petrol	36		9'9"	1'8"	6	wood	
HL	42822	Admiralty	Admiralty	Swanwick	1943	"	"	36		"	"	"	wood	
HL	42823	Admiralty	Admiralty	Swanwick	1943	"	"	36		"	"	"	wood	
HL	42824	Admiralty	Admiralty	Swanwick	1943	"	"	36		"	"	"	wood	
HL	42825	Admiralty	Admiralty	Swanwick	1943	"	"	36		"	"	"	wood	
HL	42826	Admiralty	Admiralty	Swanwick	1943	"	"	36		"	"	"	wood	
HL	43607	Admiralty	Admiralty	Swanwick	1944	20/8/43	"	36		"	"	"	wood	
HL	43608	Admiralty	Admiralty	Swanwick	1944	"	"	36		"	"	"	wood	
HL	43609	Admiralty	Admiralty	Swanwick	1944	"	"	36		"	"	"	wood	
HL	43610	Admiralty	Admiralty	Swanwick	1944	20/8/43	"	36		"	"	"	wood	
HL	43611	Admiralty	Admiralty	Swanwick	1944	"	"	36		"	"	"	wood	
HL	63612	Admiralty	Admiralty	Swanwick	1944	"	"	36		"	"	"	wood	
HL	43613	Admiralty	Admiralty	Swanwick	1944	"	"	36		"	"	"	wood	
HL	43614	Admiralty	Admiralty	Swanwick	1944	"	"	36		"	"	"	wood	
MC	43705	Admiralty	Admiralty	Swanwick	1944	7/9/43	Dorman4DSM Diesel	32		8'7"	1'7"	3.5	wood	Yes
MC	43706	Admiralty	Admiralty	Swanwick	1944	"	"	32		"	"	"	wood	
MC	43707	Admiralty	Admiralty	Swanwick	1944	"	"	32		"	"	"	wood	
MC	43708	Admiralty	Admiralty	Swanwick	1944	"	"	32		"	"	"	wood	
MC	43709	Admiralty	Admiralty	Swanwick	1944	"	"	32		"	"	"	wood	
MC	43710	Admiralty	Admiralty	Swanwick	1944	"	"	32		"	"	"	wood	
MC	43711	Admiralty	Admiralty	Swanwick	1944	"	"	32		"	"	"	wood	
MC	43712	Admiralty	Admiralty	Swanwick	1944	"	"	32		"	"	"	wood	
MC	43713	Admiralty	Admiralty	Swanwick	1944	"	"	32		"	"	"	wood	

Type	No	Owner	Designer	Place of build	Year	Order date	Engine	LOA	LWL	Beam	Draft	Tons	Material	Photo
MC	43714	Admiralty	Admiralty	Swanwick	1944	"		32					wood	
MC	43715	Admiralty	Admiralty	Swanwick	1944	"		32		"	"	"	wood	
MC	43716	Admiralty	Admiralty	Swanwick	1944	"		32		"	"	"	wood	
HL	441670	Admiralty	Admiralty	Swanwick	1945	23/10/44	VosperV8 petrol	36		10.4"	1'9"	5	wood	
HL	441671	Admiralty	Admiralty	Swanwick	1945	"	"	36		"	"	"	wood	
HL	441672	Admiralty	Admiralty	Swanwick	1945	"	"	36		"	"	"	wood	
HL	441673	Admiralty	Admiralty	Swanwick	1945	"	"	36		"	"	"	wood	
HL	44276	Admiralty	Admiralty	Swanwick	1945	10/15/44	Berguis F4 petrol	36		9'9"	1'8"	6	wood	
HL	44277	Admiralty	Admiralty	Swanwick	1945	"	"	36		"	"	"	wood	
HL	44278	Admiralty	Admiralty	Swanwick	1945	"	"	36		"	"	"	wood	
HL	44279	Admiralty	Admiralty	Swanwick	1945	"	"	36		"	"	"	wood	
HL	44280	Admiralty	Admiralty	Swanwick	1945	"	"	36		"	"	"	wood	
HL	44281	Admiralty	Admiralty	Swanwick	1945	"	"	36		"	"	"	wood	
MC	44902	Admiralty	Admiralty	Swanwick	1945	01/18/44	Dorman 4 DSM Diesel	32		8'7"	1'7"	3.5	wood	
MC	44903	Admiralty	Admiralty	Swanwick	1945	"	"	32		"	"	"	wood	
MC	44904	Admiralty	Admiralty	Swanwick	1945	"	"	32		"	"	"	wood	
MC	44905	Admiralty	Admiralty	Swanwick	1945	"	"	32		"	"	"	wood	
MC	44906	Admiralty	Admiralty	Swanwick	1945	"	"	32		"	"	"	wood	
MC	44907	Admiralty	Admiralty	Swanwick	1945	"	"	32		"	"	"	wood	
MC	44908	Admiralty	Admiralty	Swanwick	1945	"	"	32		"	"	"	wood	
MC	44909	Admiralty	Admiralty	Swanwick	1945	"	"	32		"	"	"	wood	
MC	44910	Admiralty	Admiralty	Swanwick	1945	"	"	32		"	"	"	wood	
MC	44911	Admiralty	Admiralty	Swanwick	1945	"	"	32		"	"	"	wood	
MC	44912	Admiralty	Admiralty	Swanwick	1945	"	"	32		"	"	"	wood	
MC	44913	Admiralty	Admiralty	Swanwick	1945	"	"	32		"	"	"	wood	
HL	45991	Admiralty	Admiralty	Swanwick	1947	23/6/45	VosperV8 petrol	36		9'9"	1'8"	6	wood	
HL	45992	Admiralty	Admiralty	Swanwick	1947	"		36		"	"	"	wood	
NST	54189	Admiralty	Admiralty	Swanwick		1954	PerkinsP4M diesel	39'5"		12'6"	2'4"	19.2	wood	Yes
NST	54190	Admiralty	Admiralty	Swanwick		1954	"	"		"	"	"	wood	
NST	54191	Admiralty	Admiralty	Swanwick		1954	"	"		"	"	"	wood	
NST	54192	Admiralty	Admiralty	Swanwick		1954	"	"		"	"	"	wood	
LCA	23	Admiralty	Admiralty	Swanwick	00.07.40		2xFordV8 petrol	41'6"		10'	2.25'	9-13	wood	Yes
LCA	24	Admiralty	Admiralty	Swanwick	00.07.40		"	"		"	"	"	wood	
LCA	33	Admiralty	Admiralty	Swanwick	28.08.40		"	"		"	"	"	wood	
LCA	34	Admiralty	Admiralty	Swanwick	30.08.40		"	"		"	"	"	wood	
LCA	35	Admiralty	Admiralty	Swanwick	03.10.40		"	"		"	"	"	wood	
LCA	36	Admiralty	Admiralty	Swanwick	03.10.40		"	"		"	"	"	wood	
LCA	78	Admiralty	Admiralty	Swanwick	22.11.40		"	"		"	"	"	wood	
LCA	79	Admiralty	Admiralty	Swanwick	22.11.40		"	"		"	"	"	wood	
LCA	80	Admiralty	Admiralty	Swanwick	28.11.40		"	"		"	"	"	wood	
LCA	81	Admiralty	Admiralty	Swanwick	09.12.40		"	"		"	"	"	wood	

Yacht Name	Yard	Owner	Designer	Place of Build	Year	Type	Engine	LOA ft	LWL ft	Beam ft	Draft ft	Sail Area sq.ft	Tons	Material	Photo
Cohoe		Adlard Coles	K.H.Reimers	Swanwick	1946	Aux Slp	2 cyl Stuart Turner Petrol	32	25.5	7.5	5	340	7	wood	yes
Linnet		G.N. Percival-Humphries			1946	Aux Cutt	4cyl Parsons Petrol	31.5	22	8.5	4.2	322	6	wood	
Glaramara		Sir Philip Bowyer-Smyth BT	F.Shepherd MINA	Swanwick	1947	Aux Berm Ketch	2cyl Aisla Craig Diesel	50.8	38.5	12	7.2	983	24	wood	
Chantek		O.T.Faulkner CMG	O.T.Faulkner CMG	Swanwick	1947	Aux Centre board ketch	4cyl Bergins Petrol	36.6	30.6	10.1	4	530	14	wood	
Drolene II [Britanny class]		W.G. & J.H. Gill	Laurent Giles & Partners Ltd	Swanwick	1948	Aux Berm Sloop	1 cyl Stuart Turner Petrol	31.4	25	8.2	5.3	475	8	wood	yes
Maid of York		Lt Col N.B.S Birch	Laurent Giles & Partners Ltd	Swanwick	1948	Aux Berm Sloop	2 cyl Stuart Turner Petrol	33	25.2	8.2	5.3	475	8	wood	
Pocahontas		R. Plunkett-Green	Laurent Giles & Partners Ltd	Swanwick	1948	Aux Berm Sloop	1cyl Stuart Turner Petrol	31.1	24	7.5	5.9	465	7	wood	yes
Fandango		Maj. Gen E. W. Potter MC	Laurent Giles& Partners Ltd	Swanwick	1949	Berm Sloop		43.2	33	9.1	7.2	643	12	wood	yes
Kokanee		D.D. Capper	K.H.Reimers	Swanwick	1950	Aux sloop	2cyl Stuart Turner Petrol	32.4	25.5	7.5	5	340	7	wood	
Martin-Pecheur		T.W.Holland	Arthur C. Robb	Swanwick	1950	Aux Lugger	2cyl Stuart Turner petrol	24.6	21	8.25	3.2	200	6	wood	
Ann Speed [Lion class]		John Lewis Partnership SC	Arthur C. Robb	Swanwick	1951	Aux Berm Sloop	2cyl Stuart Turner Petrol	35	24	8.75	5.5	480	9	wood	
Anna		Edward J. Freer	W.L. Hobbs MINA	Swanwick	1952	Aux Berm Sloop	1cyl 4bhp Stuart Turner petrol	22.5	17	6.5	4	208	4	wood	yes
Zaida [Lion class]		G. Colin Ratsey	Arthur C. Robb MBE	Swanwick	1952	Aux Berm Sloop	2cyl 8bhp Stuart Turner petrol	35	25	8.75	5.5	480	9	wood	
Josephine IV		Cosby Smallpiece	McGruer & Co Ltd	Swanwick	1953	Int Class 8 mtr Berm Slp		39	27.8	8.7	6.3		10	wood	yes
Half Pint [Lion class]		J.A.L. Archer	Arthur C. Robb	Swanwick	1953	Aux Berm Sloop	2cyl 8bhp Stuart Turner Petrol	35	24	8.75	5.5	480	9	wood	
Norlethe		Ronald R. Burton	Frederick R Parker MINA	Swanwick	1954	Aux Berm Sloop	4cyl 10/24bhp Ford Parsons Petrol	42.75	32.5	10.1	7.2	675	15	wood	yes
Sabeema [Lion class]		John Lewis Partnership SC	Arthur C. Robb MBE	Swanwick	1954	Aux Berm Sloop	2cyl 8bhp Stuart Turner Petrol	35	24	8.9	5.5	480	9	wood	
Leonita [Lion class]		F.M.Brown	Arthur C Robb MBE	Swanwick	1955	Aux Sloop	2cyl 10bhp Albin petrol	35	24	8.9	5.5	480	9	wood	
Marguerita Helena [Lion class] LBS 1955		Mrs. M.H. Godden Cheltenham Ltd	Arthur C. Robb MBE	Swanwick	1956	Aux Sloop	2cyl 8bhp Stuart Turner petrol	35	24	8.9	5.5	480	9	wood	yes
Moonspray		Royal Bath Hotel Bournemouth Ltd	Frederick R. Parker MINA	Swanwick	1956	Aux Sloop	4cyl 10/24 BHP Parsons petrol	40	30	9.75	6.3	578	12	wood	yes
Nyala of St Vincent LBS 1957		C. de B Barnard	Frederick R. Parker MINA	Swanwick	1956	Aux Sloop	4cyl 10/24bhp Parsons petrol	40	30	9.75	6.3	578	12	wood	
Sally Forth LBS 1958		J. Stanley Beard JP FRIBA	Frederick R. Parker MINA	Swanwick	1957	Aux Berm slp ctre plate	4cyl 10/24bhp Parsons petrol	37.5	27.5	10.75	4 plate up	600	14	wood	yes
Sardonyx		Harold F. Edwards	Frederick R. Parker MINA	Swanwick	6/57	Aux Sloop	4cyl 19bhp Ford Petrol	40	30	7.75	6.25	620	13	wood	yes
Marguerita Helena		Mrs. M.H.Godden	Frederick R. Parker MINA	Swanwick	8/57	Aux Sloop	4cyl 10/24 bhp Parson petrol	47	34.5	11.3	7	900	20	wood	yes

Yacht Name	Yard	Owner	Designer	Place of Build	Year	Type	Engine	LOA ft	LWL ft	Beam ft	Draft ft	Sail Area sq.ft	Tons	Material	Photo
Pym		D.J.Boyer DFC	Robert Clark Ltd	Swanwick	1958	Aux Sloop	Coventry Victor Petrol	37.4	27	9	6.3	600	12	wood	yes
Brynhilde		H.Dick Broom MBE	Frederick R. Parker MINA	Swanwick	7/58	Aux Sloop	2cyl 8bhp Stuart Turner petrol	32.5	24	8	5.7	4.3	7	wood	yes
Orthops LBS 1959		Hugh Orr	Robert Clark Ltd	Swanwick	9/58	Aux Sloop	2cyl 14/16bhp	36	26	9.5	4.75	546	11	wood	yes
Contango		Ivone Kinross	C.A. Nicholson	Swanwick	1959	Aux Sloop	Coventry Victor 2cyl	35	25	8.9	5.8	603	9	wood	yes
Jolina Class Felise		F.B.Lynch	C.A. Nicholson	Swanwick	1959	Aux Sloop	2cyl 14/16/bhp Coventry Victor Petrol	39	30	9.8	6.75		13	wood	
Mia [Mia design]		Dr.F.E.Ellis	Laurent Giles & Partners Ltd	Swanwick	4/60	Aux cutter	4cyl 30bhp	43	33.3	10.9	6	693	17	wood	yes
Rhiamon [Swanwick Motor cruiser]		Maj. I.B.Ramsdon MBE	Frederick Parker MINA	Swanwick	2/59	twin screw motor yacht	2x 4cyl Perkins Diesels	32.5	30.5	10	3.5		12	wood	yes
Silver Bay		Sir Guy Ropner	Frederick R. Parker MINA	Swanwick	1959	twin screw motor yacht	2x 6cyl Perkins Diesel	37.5	35	11.25	3.5		16	wood	
Toretta		P.James Agg	Robert Clark Ltd	Swanwick	8/59	Aux sloop	2cyl 14/16bhp Coventry Victor Petrol	36.8	26	9.5	4.75	546	11	wood	yes
Joannah [Solent cruiser]		Basil C.S. Hordern	Frederick R. Parker MINA	Swanwick	1959	Twin Screw Motor Yacht	2x 4cyl 22/50bhp Penta Petrol	26	24.2	8.5	2.35		6	wood	yes
Lady Winsome [Solent cruiser] LBS 1958		Lt Col Russell Naylor	Frederick R Parker MINA	Swanwick	1959	Single screw Motor yacht	4cyl 10/24 BHP Parsons petrol	26	24.5	8.5	2.35		6	wood	
Lobie II [Mia design]		Maj. K.G. Wilby	Laurent Giles & Partners Ltd	Swanwick	7/60	Aux cutter	4cyl 30bhp Thorneycroft	43.3	33.3	10.9	6	593	17	wood	
Small Fortune		A.E.Bristow	Frederick R Parker MINA	Swanwick	7/60	twin screw Motor yacht	2x 6cyl 100bhp Perkins diesels	37.5	35	11.3	3.5		17	wood	
Swan of Beaulieu LBS 1960		W.R.Clarkson	Frederick R Parker MINA	Swanwick	1960	Aux Sloop	4cyl 33/41bhp Perkins diesel	41	31	10.8	6.25	636	15	wood	
Blue Seal [Solent cruiser]		F.R.Parker	Frederick R Parker MRINA	Swanwick	1960	Twin Screw Motor Yacht	2x4cyl 70bhp Penta Petrol	26	24.2	8.5	2.3		6	wood	
Silver Spray LBS 1960		B.K.Taylor	Cox & Haswell Ltd	Swanwick	1960	twin Screw Motor Yacht	2x3cyl 100bhp Rootes Lister Diesel	32.6	29	10.6	2.75			wood	yes
Matambu	414	D.E.P. Norton	Robert Clark Ltd	Swanwick	1961	Aux Sloop	2cyl 9/16 Coventry Victor Petrol	37.4	27.9	9.5	6.4		13	wood	
Micia [Mia design]	412	Conte .Dott.Raimondo Visconti di Modroni	Laurent Giles & Partners Ltd	Swanwick	1961	Aux Cutter	4cyl 30bhp	43	33	10.8	7	693	17	wood	
Varen	411	Maj. M.S.B. Vernon MVO	GL Watson & Co	Swanwick	1/5/61	Aux Sloop	4cyl 20bhp Bergius Diesel	41.6	31.6	10.5	6.25	708	15	wood	yes
Le Cygne [Swanwick Motor cruiser]	418	E.J. Holder	Frederick R Parker MRINA	Swanwick	1961	Twin Screw Sloop	2x4cyl 30bhp Perkins diesel	32.5	30.7	10	4	140	11	wood	
Martinus	416	J.R.P. Martin	Frederick R Parker MRINA	Swanwick	1962	Twin Screw ketch	2x 6 cyl 127bhp Gardner diesel	61.5	55.3	15.8	6.5	1100	55	wood	yes
Killicrankie LBS 1962	415	B. Kilpatrick	Frederick R. Parker MRINA	Swanwick	4/62	Aux Sloop	4cyl 10/24 bhp Parsons petrol	35.5	26.5	9.5	6	492	10	wood	yes

Yacht Name	Yard	Owner	Designer	Place of Build	Year	Type	Engine	LOA ft	LWL ft	Beam ft	Draft ft	Sail Area sq.ft	Tons	Material	Photo
Maenad	417	Mrs. N.B.M. St.C. Mallison	Frederick R Parker MRINA	Swanwick	6/62	Aux Sloop	4cyl 10/24bhp Parsons petrol	41.8	31.3	10.1	6.8	700	13	wood	yes
Water Wagtail	419	L.C. & P.M. Trevelyan	Frederick R. Parker MRINA	Swanwick	1962	Twin Screw Motor yacht	2x6cyl 100bhp Perkins diesel	40.1	36.25	12	3.5		21	wood	
Piscis of Towy	420	Maj T.V. Fisher-Hoch	Frederick R. Parker MRINA	Swanwick	6/63	Twin screw Sloop	2x6cyl 82bhp Perkins diesel	37.8	35.8	11	4	410	16	wood	yes
Morning Glory	421	E.M.Brinkman	Frederick R. Parker MRINA	Swanwick	6/63	Twin screw Motor Yacht	2x4cyl 71bhp Gardiner diesels	37	34	11.5	4	200	17	wood	
Josephine VI	422	Cosby Smallpiece	Camper and Nicholson	Swanwick	6/63	Aux sloop	4cyl 116hp Coventry Victor Petrol	36	26	9.5	5.9	669	11	GRP moulded Halmatic	
Melita	424	Wing Com. R.G. Grant-Ferris MP	Laurent Giles & Partners Ltd	Swanwick	1963	Twin screw Motor yacht	2x 6cyl 84bhp Gardner Diesel	58.25	53.5	14	4.8		46	Wood	yes
Majala	427	M.J.Lanham	Frederick R. Parker MRINA	Swanwick	4/63	Aux Ketch	4cyl 47bhp Perkins Diesel	44.2	39	12.5	7	923	26	wood	
Golden Heart		Mr and Mrs. D.G. Howitt	Leslie Bowes Associates RINA	Swanwick	1963	twin screw motor sailer ketch	2x6cyl 170BHP Ajax diesels	64.9	54.6	16.6	7	1400	68	steel by Fairmile Constr.	
Bouledogue IV LBS 1964	423	J.F.Muers	Frederick R Parker MRINA	Swanwick	1/3/64	Twin screw motor yacht	2x4cyl 65bhp Gardner Diesel	43.5	40	12	4.75		23	wood	
Ketos	426	J.F.Jarvis	J.Francis Jones Associates RINA MSIA	Swanwick	1964	single screw motor yacht steadying sail	6cyl 94bhp Gardner diesels	44	40	13	5		28	wood	yes
OO-La Lah	425	F.M. Brown	Frederick R. Parker MRINA	Swanwick	8/64	Twin screw Motor yacht	2x6cyl 105bhp Perkins diesel	46	42.5	13.2	3.9		29	wood	yes
Donzella LBS 1965		Mrs&Mrs M.A. Taylor	Frederick R Parker MRINA	Warsash	1965	Twin screw motor yacht	2x6cyl 120 bhp Perkins diesels	33.75	30.7	10.8	2.75		13	wood	yes
Firedancer LBS 1965 Tormentor class	428	D.S & E.R Cottell	C.R. Holman	Swanwick	3/65	Aux sloop	4cyl 36bhp Perkins diesel	41.7	30	10.7	6.5	700	16	wood	yes
Truff	429	J.B.Barrett	Frederick R Parker MRINA	Warsash	1965	Twin screw motor yacht	2x6cyl 83 BHP Volvo Penta	26	23	10	1.6		9	wood	
Josephine VII [Hestia class] LBS 1966	430	Cosby Smallpiece	Sparkman & Stephens inc	Swanwick	1965	Aux sloop	2cyl 12bhp Arona diesel	36	25.5	9.6	6	550		wood	yes
Lame	431	R.A. Marryat	Frederick R. Parker MRINA	Swanwick	1/9/65	Aux sloop	4cyl 27bhp Perkins diesel	49	38	12.2	7	1100	23	wood	yes
Sonsie	434	Richard McDougal	John G Alden	Swanwick	1966	Aux sloop	4 cyl 120bhp Mercedes Benz diesel	36	25	10.5	4.75	517	13	GRP Moulded Halmatic	
Suchjupati	437	Paul E Penfold MVO	Arthur C. Robb MBE	Swanwick	1/7/66	Aux Ketch	4cyl 72 BHP Perkins diesel	50	37.5	13	8.3	1033	28	wood inpart A.W. Clark	
Spring Dawn Express cruiser LBS 1966		P.C. Wadham	Frederick R, Parker MRINA	Warsah	1966	Twin screw motor yacht	2x 6cyl 150bhp Volvo Penta petrol	28.6	25.5	10.5	1.7		11	wood	yes
Mabel Amelia	432	Cpt D. Mc Manus R.E B.C. Mc Manus	C.R. Holman	Swanwick	4/66	Aux sloop	4cyl 30 bhp Perkins diesel	41.7	30	10.7	6.5	700	16	wood	
unnmaed LBS 1966	436		Graham Moody	Warsash	1/12/66	clinker planked launch								wood	
Mr Moody LBS 1966	438		Graham Moody	Warsash	3/67	"								wood	
Joanine	439	Spar Holdings Ltd	Frederick R Parker Ltd	Swanwick	2/67	Twin screw motor yacht	2x6cyl 1127bhp Gardner diesel	65.6	59.6	16	5.6		62	Steel Joyce Marine	

Yacht Name	Yard	Owner	Designer	Place of Build	Year	Type	Engine	LOA ft	LWL ft	Beam ft	Draft ft	Sail Area sq.ft	Tons	Material	Photo
Firedancer of Hamble	445	D.S. Cottell	Frederick R. Parker Ltd	Swanwick	1968	Aux ketch	6cyl 164 BHP Perkins diesel	47	37	13.4	6.8	754	20	wood	yes
Murgee	447	J.L.Leroy	J.Francis Jones ARINA FRSA MRINA	Swanwick	1967	Motor sailer	6cyl 95hp Perkins diesel	45	38	13.25	5.7	1052	30	wood	
Windrush	473	Thames Conservancy		Swanwick	1/5/69	treble skin teak motor launch								wood	
Swandancer	458	Peter W. Allsebrook	Frederick R Parker Ltd	Swanwick	1/8/70	Aux ketch motor sailer	6cyl 105 bhp Thorneycroft diesel	53	45	14	6.5	947	37	wood	yes
Viamaris	469	Dr. F.E.Ellis	Laurent Giles & Partners Ltd	Swanwick	1/3/72	Aux ketch motor sailer	6cyl 94bhp Mercedes Benz Diesel	50.9	37.1	12.5	6.5	944	25	alluminium alloy W.Hewsman	
Samantha	503	Knud Hansen	McLeer and Morris	Swanwick	1/3/72	Aux. Ketch Motor sailer	6cyl 138bhp Lister Blackstone Diesel	52.5	46.1	15.2	5.9		41	GRP Halmatic Ltd	
White Wings of Topsham		S.L. Allen	Nova 27 design	Swanwick	1972	Aux sloop	1cyl 10hp Volvo Penta diesel	27	24.2	9	3	350	7	GRP Marine Construction	
Noryema IX	532	R.W. Amey	Sparkman & Stevens Inc	Swanwick	1973	Aux sloop Ocean racer	3cyl 36 bhp Volvo Penta Diesel	52.5	40	14.1	7			Alluminium W. Hewsman	
Susanne V	538	Herr S. Wessel	Laurent Giles & Partners Ltd	Swanwick	1/8/74	Deck saloon Motor sailer ketch	2 x6cyl 140 BHP Perkins diesel	63	48	16.5	8	1621	53	GRP Halmatic	
Noryema	532	R.W. Amey	German Freres	Swanwick	1/5/75	Aux sloop Ocean Racer	4cyl 75bhp Volvo Penta Diesel	46.2	37.7	13.3	7.5	996	28	Alloy Joyce Marine	
Bonaire	556	Olbia Ltd	Laurent Giles & Partners Ltd	Swanwick	1/4/77	Moody 66 Raised saloon Motor sailer Ketch	V8 140bhp Perkins	65.3	50.5	16.1	8.2	1621	53	GRP Halmatic Ltd	
Morning Cloud Sail no 2468	577	Rt. Hon. Edward Heath MBE MP	Ron Holland	Swanwick	1/5/77	Ocean racer Aux sloop	3cyl 30bhp Lister diesel	43.9	36.8	13.3	7.8		17.87	Alloy Martland Marine	yes
Princess Irene	550	Ray Turner	Laurent Giles & Partners Ltd	Swanwick	1/2/77	Deck Saloon ketch	2x 6cyl 95bhp diesel	60	49.5	15.6	7.8	1850	48	Alluminium W.Hewsman	
Salar 40															
Salmo Salar LBS 1966	435	Air Vice Marshall E.L. Colbeck-Welsh CB OBE DFC RAF	Laurent Giles & Partners Ltd	Swanwick	1/2/65	Auxillery motor sailer	4 cyl 62/72 bhp Perkins diesel	39	31	11.4	5.25	550	19	Wood	yes
Dorcelle LBS 1966	440	D.W. Morrell	"	"	1/9/66	"	"	"	"	"			"		
Delfin Salar		John David	"	Warsash	1966	"	"	"	"	""			"		
Lady Kate		Chichester Marine Electronics Ltd	"	"	12/66	"	"	"	"	"			17	GRP Kemp & Pitt	
Gander		T.B.D. Kendal	"	"	1966	"	"	"	"	"	"	"	"	"	
Serifa		R.S.Shaw	"	"	1967	"	"	"	"	"	"	"	"	"	
Sinbad the Salar		S.Kilpatrick		"	6/67	"	"	"	"	"	"	"	"	"	
Halberdier 36															
Meribelle II LBS 1967	444	Dr JB & Mrs MH Shield MB FRCS	Alan F Hill	Swanwick	1/3/67	Centre cockpit dog house mtr slr ketch	4cyl 35hp Perkins 4.107 diesel	36.1	28	11.1	5	611	16	GRP Marine Construction	yes

Yacht Name	Yard	Owner	Designer	Place of Build	Year	Type	Engine	LOA ft	LWL ft	Beam ft	Draft ft	Sail Area sq.ft	Tons	Material	Photo
Salvo	448	J.Jarvis	"	Swanwick	1/4/67	"	"	"	"	"	"	"	15	"	
Nylmec	449	E.O. Celwyn-Jones	"	"	1/7/67	"	"	"	"	"	"	"	15	"	
Sabrewing	452	D.J. Norton	"	"	1/8/67	"	"	"	"	"	"	"	13	"	
Shamrock	453	Knud Hansen	"	"	1/8/67	"	"	"	"	"	"	"	13	"	
Bellrock II	455	Mr.& Mrs.T.S.Passmore	"	"	1/3/68	"	"	"	"	"	"	"	13	"	
LBS 1968															
Lindos	454	W.R & B. E. Hamilton	"	"	1/4/68	"	"	"	"	"	"	"	13	"	
Crisanda	459	A. Chris Bryant	"	"	1/4/68	"	"	"	"	"	"	"	13	"	
Sun Venture	456	G.F.& K.O. Simms	"	"	1/4/68	"	"	"	"	"	"	"	15	"	
Alerica	460	E.G.F. Knowles	"	"	1/5/68	"	"	"	"	"	"	"	13	"	
Jabberwock III	461	Mr & Mrs C.D. Skinner	"	"	1/6/68	"	"	"	"	"	"	"	13	"	
Navajo X	462	H. Lemm	"	"	1/6/68	"	"	"	"	"	"	"	16	"	
Tremolino	463	G. Allen	"	"	1/7/68	"	"	"	"	"	"	"	15	"	
Cindus	464	W.F.Price & Co	"	"	1/8/68	"	"	"	"	"	"	"	13	"	
Bolleann	465	C. A. Brindle	"	"	1/9/68	"	"	"	"	"	"	"	13	"	
Maxine	466	M. Faiman	"	"	1/10/68	"	"	"	"	"	"	"	15	"	
Hazana	467	G. H. Chaplain	"	"	1/5/69	"	"	"	"	"	"	"	15	"	
Unnamed	469	exported to USA	"	"	1/1/69	"	"	"	"	"	"	"	"	"	
Maridadi	470	G.Crowther	"	"	1/3/69	"	"	"	"	"	"	"	14	"	
LBS 1969															
Gorgeous	471	A.W.A. Rundle	"	"	1/3/69	"	"	"	"	"	"	"	15	"	
Sarva of Beaulieu	474	Mr & Mrs P.E.J. Hunt	"	"	1/5/69	"	"	"	"	"	"	"	14	"	
Nerin	475	Mr & Mrs W.E. Johnson	"	"	1/6/69	"	"	"	"	"	"	"	14	"	
Arbaleste	476	D. A. Coaker	"	"	1/8/69	"	"	"	"	"	"	"	14	"	
Belle Mere	477	M.F. Beckett	"	"	1/7/69	"	"	"	"	"	"	"	14	"	
Timsdal	478	Werner Weber	"	"	1/10/69	"	"	"	"	"	"	"	15	"	
Lanceolate	479	P.J.Reeves	"	"	1/5/70	"	"	"	"	"	"	"	13	"	
Espera	483	R.G. Coleman	"	"	1/9/70	"	"	"	"	"	"	"	13	"	
Madrisa	484	Stanley Smith	"	"	1/4/71	"	"	"	"	"	"	"	15	"	
Sareliza	490	Peter Jones	"	"	1/4/71	"	"	"	"	"	"	"	13	"	
LBS 1971															
Halberd	501	W Stockdale	"	"	1/8/71	"	"	"	"	"	"	"	15	"	
Hyperion of Hamble	502	R. Roskell	"	"	1/5/72	"	"	"	"	"	"	"	15	"	
Part Ass.	516		"	"		"	"	"	"	"	"	"	"	"	
Ragtime Part Ass	555	R.F.G. Morrison			1/5/75	"	"	"	"	"	"	"	"	"	
Cavalier 36															
Moody Maid	485	W. Stockdale	Alan F Hill	Swanwick	1/6/70	Deck saloon Motor sailer Aft cockpit sloop	4cyl 35bhp Perkins 4.107 Diesel	36.1	28	11.1	5	572	13	GRP Marine Construction	yes
Gay Cavalier	486	B.Colenzo	"	"	1/4/70	"	"	"	"	"	"	"	"	"	
Xim	489	J.P.Stacey TD FRICS	"	"	1/6/70	"	"	"	"	"	"	"	"	"	
Salvo	491	J. Jarvis	"	"	1/6/70	"	"	"	"	"	"	"	"	"	
Koala	494	S.P.Higgin	"	"	1/8/70	"	"	"	"	"	"	"	"	"	
Loladue	497	P. Friedenberg	"	"	1/10/70	"	"	"	"	"	"	"	"	"	
Maria Mia	498	Trident Petroleum	"	"	1/7/71	"	"	"	"	"	"	"	"	"	
Part Ass.	460		"	"	1/11/76	"	"	"	"	"	"	"	"	"	
Carbineer 44															
Corrival	468	Mr & Mrs GHR Watson	Laurent Giles& Partners Ltd	Swanwick	1/6/69	Carbineer 44 deck saloon Motor sailer	6cyl 95bhp Perkins diesel	44	36	12.2	6	850	22	GRP Marine Construction	yes
LBS 1969															
Ceol Mara	480	Lt.Com D.G.Silcock DSC RNR	"	"	1/11/69	"	"	"	"	"	"	"	"	"	

Yacht Name	Yard	Owner	Designer	Place of Build	Year	Type	Engine	LOA ft	LWL ft	Beam ft	Draft ft	Sail Area sq.ft	Tons	Material	Photo
Calibre	481	D.J. Norton	"	"	1/5/70	"	"	"	"	"	"	"	"	"	
Mutineer	487	C.J.Sanders	"	"	1/4/71	"	"	"	"	"	"	"	"	"	
		Taken over by Sqr.Ldr N Duke													
Dorothee	492	Cpt.H. Bert Heinen	"	"	1/9/70	"	"	"	"	"	"	"	"	"	
Altair	493	Betelguese YC Ltd	"	"	1/9/70	"	"	"	"	"	"	"	"	"	
Twirlybird	495	A. Bristow	"	"	1/4/71	"	"	"	"	"	"	"	"	"	
Abra	405	Mr.& Mrs D.B. Hulme	"	"	1/9/71	"	"	"	"	"	"	"	"	"	
Susanne IV	500	Mr Wessel	"	"	1971	"	"	"	"	"	"	"	"	"	
Waterbird	505	GM & GEJ Deering	"	"	1/6/72	"	"	"	"	"	"	"	"	"	
Carronade of Rhu	507	Mr Newell taken over by Mr Viney DSO DFC	"	"	1/3/72	"	"	"	"	"	"	"	"	"	
Ardnamona	511	P.J. Langton	"	"	1/5/72	"	"	"	"	"	"	"	"	"	
Synolda	513	V.S.H. Walker	"	"	1/9/72	"	"	"	"	"	"	"	"	"	
Harvest Maid	514	C.G. Bellingham	"	"	1/11/72	"	"	"	"	"	"	"	"	"	
Moody Lady	518	Terance A. Boughton	"	"	1/3/73	"	"	"	"	"	"	"	"	"	
Carbineer 46															
Clamar	515	R.C. Pascoe	"	"	1/7/73	Carbineer 46 deck saloon Motor sailer	"	46.5	"	"	"	"	"	"	
Violante	520	G.H.Lewis	"	"	1/3/73	"	"	"	"	"	"	"	"	"	
LBS 1973															
Bonaire	521	P.J. Agg	"	"	1/4/73	"	"	"	"	"	"	"	"	"	
Martie	525	Mr Musgrave & Mr Kalis	"	"	1/11/73	"	"	"	"	"	"	"	"	"	
Barleycorn	526	R.H. Courage	"	"	1/7/73	"	"	"	"	"	"	"	"	"	
Niobe	530	P. Harper	"	"	1/9/73	"	"	"	"	"	"	"	"	"	
Hazana	533	P.G.Crompton	"	"	1/3/74	"	"	"	"	"	"	"	"	"	
LBS 1974															
Gay Dog	535	E.A.H. Furmstone	"	"	1/6/74	"	"	"	"	"	"	"	"	"	
Sareliza	537	Mr & Mrs.P Jones	"	"	1/5/74	"	"	"	"	"	"	"	"	"	
White Billow	539	H.J.Burley Smith	"	"	1/7/74	"	"	"	"	"	"	"	"	"	
Ultimate	541	J.D.Henson	"	"	1/2/75	"	"	"	"	"	"	"	"	"	
Durendal	545	Dotte.ing.g. Cardini	"	"	1/4/75	"	"	"	"	"	"	"	"	"	
Totuma II	546	Alberto Metancourt Irribarren	"	"	1/6/75	"	"	"	"	"	"	"	"	"	
Le Franglais	548	G Girard	"	"	1/10/75	"	"	"	"	"	"	"	"	"	
Santa Mavara	557	Dr.A.W.Corrado Campeis	"	"	1/5/76	"	"	"	"	"	"	"	"	"	
Untier IV	559	Ulrich Gerhart & Amalie Erhart	"	"	1/4/77	"	"	"	"	"	"	"	"	"	
Baltica II	5005	Guy. A. Weston	"	"	1/10/78	"	"	"	"	"	"	"	"	"	
Whistling Maid	576	Richmond Hotel Co.	"	"	1978	"	"	"	"	"	"	"	"	"	
Narooma	5011		"	"	1991	"	"	"	"	"	"	"	"	"	
Lancer 42															
Loch Tummel	457	B. Kilpatrick	Graham Moody	Swanwick	1/7/68	Lancer 42 Twin screw Motor Yacht	2x6cyl 95bhp Perkins diesels	42.5	38.5	12.6	3.6		25.7	GRP by Tyler Boat Company	yes
LBS 1968															
Usutu	472	R.C.U. Corbett	"	"	1/7/69	"	"	"	"	"	"	"	"	"	
Rafales	488	Mrs Molly B. Cox	"	"	1/7/70	"	"	"	"	"	"	"	"	"	

Yacht Name	Yard	Owner	Designer	Place of Build	Year	Type	Engine	LOA ft	LWL ft	Beam ft	Draft ft	Sail Area sq.ft	Tons	Material	Photo
Amida	482	Mr & Mrs Albrey Gwilym	"	"	1971	"	"	"	"	"	"	"	"	"	
Part Ass.															
Come True II	512	W.T.Eden	"	"	1/8/72	"	"	"	"	"	"	"	"	"	yes
Moody 44															
Equity of Hamble	510	Mr & Mrs D.A. Craps	Laurent Giles & Partners Ltd	Swanwick	1/4/92	Moody 44 Centre Cockpit Aux ketch	4cyl 40bhp Perkins 4-108 diesel	44	34	12.7	6.5	1000	22	GRP Halmatic Ltd	
LBS 1972															
Eccola-Ancora	517		"	"	1972	"		"	"	"	"	"	"	"	
Part Ass.															
Isolde of Hamble	519	F.M. Gill	"	"	1/9/72	"	"	"	"	"	"	"	"	"	
New Melody	522	J. Guillaume	"	"	1/9/72	"		"	"	"	"	"	"	"	
Part Ass.	523		"	"		"		"	"	"	"	"	"	"	
Part Ass.	524		"	"		"		"	"	"	"	"	"	"	
Candida	528	Klaus Girardet	"	"	1/5/73	"	"	"	"	"	"	"	"	"	
Ouzo	529	W.H.Bishop	"	"	1/4/73	"		"	"	"	"	"	"	"	
LBS 1973		G.R.C. Shaw													
Holworth lady	531	L. Coates	"	"	1/3/74	"	"	"	"	"	"	"	"	"	
LBS 1974															
Downley	534		"	"	1/7/73	Aux sloop	"	"	"	"	"	"	"	"	
Velella	536		"	"	1/6/74	Aux ketch	"	"	"	"	"	"	"	"	
Part Ass.	540		"	"		"		"	"	"	"	"	"	"	
Springhill Lady	542	Springhill Overseas Ltd	"	"	1/2/75	"	"	"	"	"	"	"	"	"	
LBS 1975															
Betty's Mink III	543	R.F.T. JOnes	"	"	1/3/75	"	"	"	"	"	"	"	"	"	
Cougar	544		"	"	1/8/75	"		"	"	"	"	"	"	"	
Part Ass.															
Westernesse	553	Mr Clayton, Fyson Pearce and Godal	"	"	1/6/75	"	"	"	"	"	"	"	"	"	
	5024		"	"	1/9/79	"	"	"	"	"	"	"	"	"	
Giles 38															
Fionn-Choix	509		Laurent Giles & Partners Ltd	Swanwick	1/4/72	Giles 38									
LBS 1972															
Part Ass.	527			"		Aux Sloop									
Moody 42															yes
Mimas	561		Angus S. Primrose	Swanwick	1/4/77	Deck saloon Ctr cockpit Ketch Motor Sailer	4cyl 72bhp Perkins 4-236 diesel	41.5	34.1	13.4	5.1	762	18.52	GRP Rober Ives Boatbuilders Ltd	
LBS 1977															
Smiling Face	562		"	"	1/4/77	"	"	"	"	"	"	"	"	"	
Asolare	563		"	"	1/4/77	"	"	"	"	"	"	"	"	"	
Carronade of Lorne	564	S.P. Newell	"	"	1/5/77	"	"	"	"	"	"	"	"	"	
Trade	565	Chantiers Vanek	"	"	1/5/77	"	"	"	"	"	"	"	"	"	
Trade	566	Intersail	"	"	1/6/77	"	"	"	"	"	"	"	"	"	
Trade	567	Kip Marina	"	"	1/9/77	"	"	"	"	"	"	"	"	"	
Arcas VII	568	W.S. Bransom	"	"	1/7/77	"	"	"	"	"	"	"	"	"	
Dawn Haze	569	H. K. Enoch	"	"	1/7/77	"	"	"	"	"	"	"	"	"	
Trade	570	Chantier Vanek	"	"	1/8/77	"	"	"	"	"	"	"	"	"	
Trade	571	Intersail	"	"	1/9/77	"	"	"	"	"	"	"	"	"	
Trade	572	Chantier Vanek	"	"	1/9/77	"	"	"	"	"	"	"	"	"	
Trade	573	Schaeffler Marine	"	"	1/9/77	"	"	"	"	"	"	"	"	"	
Kilcreggan	574	B.Kilpatrick	"	"	1/11/77	"	"	"	"	"	"	"	"	"	
Ivory Gull of Sussex	578	K.A.S.Potter	"	"	1/10/77	"	"	"	"	"	"	"	"	"	
Lady Geannette	579		"	"	1/10/77	"	"	"	"	"	"	"	"	"	
Trade	580	Kip Marina	"	"	1/10/77	"	"	"	"	"	"	"	"	"	

Yacht Name	Yard	Owner	Designer	Place of Build	Year	Type	Engine	LOA ft	LWL ft	Beam ft	Draft ft	Sail Area sq.ft	Tons	Material	Photo
Adaire	582			"	1/2/78	"	"	"	"	"	"	"	"	"	
LBS 1979															
Jolly Gulliver	575	C.W. Hutchinson	"	"	1/2/78	"	"	"	"	"	"	"	"	"	
Lorella	581	Kip Marina	"	"	1/3/78	"	"	"	"	"	"	"	"	"	
(Trade)															
Ocean Phoenix	583	C.N.Cooke	"	"	1/4/78	"	"	"	"	"	"	"	"	"	
Tumblelina	584	D.L. Campbell MC	"	"	1/4/78	"	"	"	"	"	"	"	"	"	
		C.H. Davis													
Nuthatch	586	F.M. Gill	"	"	1978	"	"	"	"	"	"	"	"	"	
Jamieson III	588		"	"	1/1/78	"	"	"	"	"	"	"	"	"	
Part Ass.	5900		"	"		"	"	"	"	"	"	"	"	"	
Escapade of Torbay	5920		"	"	1/6/78	"	"	"	"	"	"	"	"	"	
Trade	5930	Schaeffler Marine	"	"	1/9/78	"	"	"	"	"	"	"	"	"	
Kikatu	5950	G.E. Platts	"	"	1/12/78	"	"	"	"	"	"	"	"	"	
Trade	5910	Kip Marina	"	"	1/7/78	"	"	"	"	"	"	"	"	"	
Beyond	5940	W.A. & S.E. Andrews	"	"	1/10/78	"	"	"	"	"	"	"	"	"	
Rory Mor	5960	A. Howard	"	"	1/4/79	"	"	"	"	"	"	"	"	"	
Papa-Kay	5980	P.H. Kelsey	"	"	1/3/79	"	"	"	"	"	"	"	"	"	
Junica	5990		"	"	1/4/79	"	"	"	"	"	"	"	"	"	
Halvic	5970	H.V. Beer	"	"	1/3/79	"	"	"	"	"	"	"	"	"	
	5001		"	"	1/4/79	"	"	"	"	"	"	"	"	"	
Tide Cottage	5002		"	"	1/5/79	"	"	"	"	"	"	"	"	"	
Part Ass.	5009		"	"	1/8/78	"	"	"	"	"	"	"	"	"	
Kabier IV	5016		"	"	1/3/79	"	"	"	"	"	"	"	"	"	
South Wind	5017		"	"	1/4/79	"	"	"	"	"	"	"	"	"	
Spindrift of Hamble	5021		"	"	1/1/80	"	"	"	"	"	"	"	"	"	
Zooth II	5022		"	"	1/5/80	"	"	"	"	"	"	"	"	"	
Sassenach	5023	Swannay Farm Cheese Ltd	"	"	1980	"	"	"	"	"	"	"	"	"	
Martini Lad	5025	M. Menaged	"	"	1/2/80	"	"	"	"	"	"	"	"	"	
Golden Flower	5028		"	"	1/3/80	"	"	"	"	"	"	"	"	"	
Sagapo III	5029		"	"	1/4/80	"	"	"	"	"	"	"	"	"	
Golden Crow	5035		"	"	1/4/80	"	"	"	"	"	"	"	"	"	
Petronella	5040		"	"		"	"	"	"	"	"	"	"	"	
Kiribati	5042		"	"		"	"	"	"	"	"	"	"	"	
Cailyn OG	5044		"	"		Mark II	"	"	"	"	"	"	"	"	
Spellbound of Skellig	5045		"	"		Mark II	"	"	"	"	"	"	"	"	
Narcissus	5941		"	"			"	"	"	"	"	"	"	"	
Jacquelina VI	5043		"	"			"	"	"	"	"	"	"	"	
(trade)															
West Top	5048		"	"			"	"	"	"	"	"	"	"	
Tagembo III	5049			"											
Moody 379															
Trade	5026	Chantier Vanek	German Frers	Swanwick	1/1/80	Fast Aux Sloop	3cyl 36bhp Bukh diesel	37.9	31	12	6.5	695		GRP Robert Ives Boat builders Limited	yes

Yacht Name	Yard	Owner	Designer	Place of Build	Year	Type	Engine	LOA ft	LWL ft	Beam ft	Draft ft	Sail Area sq.ft	Tons	Material	Photo
Family Affair (Cassis)	5030		"	"	1/2/80		"								
Uwch-Y-Don	5031		"	"			"	"	"	"	"	"		"	
Trade Part Ass.	5051	Chantier Vanek	"	"			"	"	"	"	"	"		"	
Powells															
Dabboos	5066		Bernard Olysinske	Swanwick		Powells 46 TSDY	2x GM Detroits diesels							GRP	
Trade	5056	JPIM Hong Kong	"	"		Powells 50 TSDY								"	
Trade	5062	JPIM Hong Kong	"	"		Powells 50 TSDY	"							"	
Melrik	5068	Melrik Ltd	"	"		Powells 50 TSDY	"							"	
unnamed	5070	Middle East	"	"	1/10/83	Powells 50 TSDY	"							"	
unnamed	5075	Middle East	"	"		Powells 50 TSDY	"							"	
Trade	5057	JPIM Hong Kong	"	"		Powells 53 TSDY	"							"	
Charlotte	5074		"	"		Powells 53 TSDY	"							"	
Ribs															
Trade	5107	MOD		Swanwick	1987	28' Rib								GRP	
Trade	5108	MOD		"	"	"								"	
Trade	5109	MOD		"	"	"								"	
No name	5110	MOD		"	1993	38' Rib								"	
Grenadier 134															
Leslie Frank of Bursledon	5037		Laurent Giles & Partners Ltd	Swanwick		Open Centre Cockpit Motor sailer Ketch	4cyl 72bhp Perkins 4.236 Diesel	44	34.5	13.5	7/6.3	900	14.5	GRP Robert Ives Boatbuilders Ltd	yes
Black Watch	5038		"	"	1992	"	"	"	"	"	"	"	"	"	
Stream Tide	5039		"	"		"	"	"	"	"	"	"	"	"	
Camina	5082		"	"		"	"	"	"	"	"	"	"	"	
Navstar	5052		"	"		"	"	"	"	"	"	"	"	"	
Mystic Mood	5053		"	"		"	"	"	"	"	"	"	"	"	
Janetta Emily	5054		"	"		"	"	"	"	"	"	"	"	"	
Tiggywinkle	5055		"	"	1988	"	"	"	"	"	"	"	"	"	
Magic Drifter	5058		"	"		"	"	"	"	"	"	"	"	"	
Sassenach	5063		"	"	1983	"	"	"	"	"	"	"	"	"	
Bubble Burst	5065		"	"	1997	"	"	"	"	"	"	"	"	"	
Aclofrolic	5067		"	"		"	"	"	"	"	"	"	"	"	
Owl of Abersoch	5078		"	"		"	"	"	"	"	"	"	"	"	
Kelebek	5091		"	"		"	"	"	"	"	"	"	"	"	
Grenadier 119															
Trade	5059		Laurent Giles & Partners Ltd	Swanwick	1980	Open Centre Cockpit Motor Sailer sloop/ketch	4cyl 47bhp Perkins 4.108 Diesel	39.2	29	12.5	6'	750		GRP Robert Ives Boatbuilders Ltd	yes
Calissia	5061		"	"		"	"	"	"	"	"	"	"	"	
Sea Fantasy	5064		"	"		"	"	"	"	"	"	"	"	"	

Yacht Name	Yard	Owner	Designer	Place of Build	Year	Type	Engine	LOA ft	LWL ft	Beam ft	Draft ft	Sail Area sq.ft	Tons	Material	Photo
Moody 47															
Contango	5069		Bill Dixon	Swanwick	1982	Open Centre Cockpit	4cyl 60/66bhp	46.5	38.9	14.8	6.9	1125	Displ 27500	GRP	yes
						fast cruising	Thorneycroft						lbs	Moody	
						Sloop	Diesel								
Its got to be	5071		"	"		"	"	"	"	"	"	"	"	"	
Encola Terza	5072		"	"		"	"	"	"	"	"	"	"	"	
Part Ass															
Simha	5073		"	"		"	"	"	"	"	"	"	"	"	
Kisima	5076		"	"		"	"	"	"	"	"	"	"	"	
Kynuma	5077		"	"		"	"	"	"	"	"	"	"	"	
Caoarn	5079		"	"		"	"	"	"	"	"	"	"	"	
Solent Venture	5080		"	"		"	"	"	"	"	"	"	"	"	
Hulie	5081		"	"		"	"	"	"	"	"	"	"	"	
Vaduz	5084		"	"		"	"	"	"	"	"	"	"	"	
No name	5085		"	"		"	"	"	"	"	"	"	"	"	
Low Profile	5086		"	"		"	"	"	"	"	"	"	"	"	
Divershun	5088		"	"		"	"	"	"	"	"	"	"	"	
Trade	5089	Impex	"	"		"	"	"	"	"	"	"	"	"	
Saharco	5090		"	"	1987	"	"	"	"	"	"	"	"	"	
Rebecca of	5092		"	"	1/7/86	"	"	"	"	"	"	"	"	"	
Menai															
Novatini	5093		"	"	1986	"	"	"	"	"	"	"	"	"	
Abask	5094		"	"	1/6/86	"	"	"	"	"	"	"	"	"	
White Gazelle	5097		"	"	1987	"	"	"	"	"	"	"	"	"	
Serendipity	5098		"	"	1986	"	"	"	"	"	"	"	"	"	
of Swanwick															
Trade	5099	Chantier Vanek	"	"	1987	"	"	"	"	"	"	"	"	"	
Wild Mood						"									
Moody 471															
Nisha	5104	Nisha Ltd	"	"	1987	"	"	"	"	"	"	"	"	"	yes
Trade	5105	Yachting Austria	"	"	1987	"	"	"	"	"	"	"	"	"	
Ocean Hound	5106		"	"		"	"	"	"	"	"	"	"	"	
No name	5111		"	"	1988	"	"	"	"	"	"	"	"	"	
Moody 470															
Leopards Star	5121		Bill Dixon	Swanwick	1991	Raised saloon centre cockpit								GRP Moody	
Moody 52													tons		
Charlena	552	Peritalo Ltd	Laurent Giles & Partners Ltd	Swanwick	1/2/76	Deck saloon	6cyl 109bhp Perkins 6.354 diesel	51.9	39	14.2	6.9	1123	32	GRP Halmatic Ltd	yes
Sweet Alma of Kip	554	Mr. & Mrs D.Holt	"		1/8/76	Motor sailer ketch "	twin screw diesel engines	"	"	"	"	"	32	"	
Mirmir of Gorey	585	Mirmir Marine Ltd	"	"	1/2/78	"	6cyl 109bhp Perkins 6.354 diesel	"	"	"	"	"	"	"	
Breakaway M	5890	Mr & Mrs A.McFadden	"		1/7/78	"	"	"	"	"	"	"	32	"	
Sakase	5018		"		1979	"	"	"	"	"	"	"	"	"	
Unnamed	5018		"		1/6/79	"	"	"	"	"	"	"	"	"	
Palandra	5036		"		1/7/83	"	"	"	"	"	"	"	"	"	
Auhinga II	5027		"	"	1991	"	"	"	"	"	"	"	"	"	
Serandip	5014		"	"	1/4/79	"	"	"	"	"	"	"	"	"	

Yacht Name	Yard	Owner	Designer	Place of Build	Year	Type	Engine	LOA ft	LWL ft	Beam ft	Draft ft	Sail Area sq.ft	Tons	Material	Photo
Moody 58															
Ardent Spirit	5100		Bill Dixon	Swanwick	1988	Raised Saloon Centre Cockpit Motor Sailer sloop	6cyl 114bhp Perkins6/3544 diesel	57.5	48.1	16.4	7/5.9	1721		GRP Moody	
Unnamed Part Ass.	5101		"	"	1991	"		"	"	"	"	"		"	
Unnamed Part Ass.	5102		"	"		"		"	"	"	"	"		"	
Culverneer 500															yes
Aquilo	5112		Bill Dixon	Swanwick	1988	Raised saloon Centre Cockpit motor sailer sloop	60/66hp Thorneycroft Diesel	49.7	38.9	14.8	6.9	1125		GRP Moody	
On Business	5113		"	"	1989	"		"	"	"	"	"		"	
Unnamed	5114		"	"	1989	"		"	"	"	"	"		"	
Unnamed	5115		"	"	1989	"		"	"	"	"	"		"	
Unnamed	5118		"	"	1993	"		"	"	"	"	"		"	
Culverneer 600															
La Belciza	5120		"	"	1991		6cyl114 hp Perkins 6/3544 diesel	59.2	48.1	16.4	7'/59"	17021		GRP Moody	
Grenadier 183															
Blue Fin	5060		Laurent Giles & Partners Ltd	Swanwick	1982	Raised saloon centre cockpit	Perkins 140hp diesel	60	48	16.5	8	1021	35.5	GRP Halmatic Ltd	yes
Trawler type															
Romana G	5019		Freeward Marine Ltd	Swanwick	1/7/79	Trawler 36 Twin screw Semi Displacement	2x 6cyl 120/180bhp Ford Sabre Diesel	36	31	13	4			GRP Robert Ives Boatbuilders Ltd	
Chunky	5015		"	"	1/2/79	"	"	"	"	"	"				
Leslie Frank of Hamble	5095		Tyler	Swanwick	1986	Trawler 48 Semi displacement		48						GRP Tyler Boat Company	
Miscellaneous one-offs															
Niobe Moody39 custom	551	Peter Harper	Angus S Primrose	Swanwick	1/3/76	Centre Cockpit Motor sailer ketch	4 cyl 40bhp Perkins diesel	38.7	32.5	13.7	5.5	910	15.06	GRP Marine Projects Ltd	
Orthops of Hamble Moody 30 custom	558	Hugh Orr	Angus S Primrose	Swanwick	1/6/76	Aft cockpit Aux sloop	2cyl 25bhp Volvo Penta Diesel	29.6	26	9.7	4.7	526	711	GRP Marine Projects Ltd	
Lazy B Eclipse 43 custom	5116	R. Barton	Bill Dixon	Swanwick	1990	Deck saloon Motor sailer sloop	4cyl 78bhp Perkins M80T Diesel	42.5	36.8	9'7"	4.83			GRP Marine Projects Ltd	
Drum (fit out)	5087		Ron Holland	Swanwick	1989	Ocean racer Maxi									
Noryema	5012	Noryema Marine Ltd		Swanwick	1/2/79	Ocean racer Maxi	4cyl Perkins 72 hp diesel							Joyce Marine	

Moody Yachts jointly developed and built by Marine Projects (Plymouth) Ltd/ Princess Yachts International Ltd sold and marketed by Moody 1972 -2004

Model type	Yard No From	Build duration	Designer	Place built	No. Built	Type	Engine	LOA	LWL	Beam	Draft	Sail area sq ft	Displ	Material	Photo
Moody 33		9/1973 - 9/1978	Angus S. Primrose	Plymouth	242	Centre cockpit Aux sloop	4cyl 36bhp Perkins/Thorneycroft Diesel	33'	28.5'	11.5'	4'5" fin	580	4.69 t	GRP	Yes
Moody 30		9/1975 - 11/1979	"	"	162	Aft cockpit Aux sloop	23bhp Volvo Penta MD11C diesel	30'	26'	10'1"	4'9" fin	373	8100lb	GRP	Yes
Moody 39		12/1975 - 12/1978		"	82	Centre cockpit Aux sloop	4cyl 47bhp Thorneycroft T108 Diesel	38'6"	32'6"	13'4"	5'6"	595	18150lb	GRP	Yes
Moody 36		12/1977 - 8/1981	"	"	89	Centre Cockpit Aux sloop	4cyl 35bhp Thorneycroft T90 Diesel	36'	30'	12'4"	5'	506	14700lb	GRP	Yes
Moody 33 Mark II		9/1978 - 6/1981	"	"	121	Centre cockpit Aux sloop	4cyl 35bhp Thorneycroft T90 Diesel	33'	28'5"	11'5"	4'5" fin	580	10504lb	GRP	Yes
Moody 40		12/1978 - 8/1981	"	"	56	Centre cockpit Aux sloop	4cyl 47bhp Thorneycroft T108 diesel	39'6"	32'6"	13'4"	5'6"	595	18150lb	GRP	Yes
Moody 33S	B2010	9/1979 - 2/1982	"	"	54	Aft cockpit Aux sloop	Bukh 20bhp or 4cyl 35 bhp Thorneycroft T90 Diesel	33'	28'5"	11'5"	4'5" fin	580	10506lb	GRP	Yes
Moody29		7/1980 - 7/1983	"	"	145	Aft cockpit Aux sloop	2cyl 20bhp Bukh DV20ME Diesel	29'8"	25'	10'6"	4'6"fin 3'6"bilge	367	7300lb	GRP	Yes
Moody 36DS		9/1980 - 6/1981	"	"	4	Deck saloon Aux sloop	4cyl 35bhp Thorneycroft Diesel	36'	30'	12'4"	5'	506	14700lb	GRP	Yes
Moody 36S		9/1981 - 3/1983	Angus Primrose	Plymouth	19	Aft cockpit Aux sloop	4cyl 35bhp Thorneycroft T90 diesel	36	30	12'4"	5'	506	14700lb	GRP	Yes
Moody 333		9/1981 - 8/1983	"	"	77	Centre Cockpit Aux sloop	4cyl 35bhp Thorneycroft T90 Diesel	33'	28'5"	11'5"	4'9" fin	608	10575lb	GRP	Yes
Moody41	D3010	12/1981 - 8/1984	Bill Dixon	Plymouth	53	Centre Cockpit Aux sloop	4cyl 48bhp Thorneycroft T108 diesel	41'	34'	13'2"	6' fin	954	20600lb	GRP	Yes
Moody 27	F1010	12/1981 - 8/1985	"	"	162	Aft cockpit Aux sloop	17bhp/18bhp Volvo Penta Diesel	27'8"	21'11"	9'8"	4'8" fin 3'5"bilge	412	5750lb	GRP	Yes
Moody 34	G1010	6/1983 - 6/1986	"	"	165	Centre cockpit Aux sloop	4cyl 35bhp Thorneycroft T90 or Volvo Penta 28bhp Diesel	33'5"	27'9"	11'8"	5'fin 3'9"bilge	514	11200lb	GRP	Yes
Moody 31 Mark I & II	E2010	9/1983-6/1991	"	"	305	Aft cockpit Aux sloop	28bhp Volvo Penta2003 Diesel	30.75	25.42	10.5	5'fin 3.7bilge	503	9966lb	GRP	Yes

Model type	Yard No From	Build duration	Designer	Place built	No. Built	Type	Engine	LOA	LWL	Beam	Draft	Sail area sq ft	Displ	Material	Photo
Moody 419		8/1984 - 7/1986	"		60	Centre cockpit Aux sloop	4cyl 50bhp Thorneycroft T108 diesel	41'9"	33'11"	13'2"	6'fin	954	20600lb	GRP	Yes
Moody 37/376	C8010	7/1985 - 8/1991	"		313	Centre cockpit Aux sloop	4cyl 35/47bhp Thorneycroft T90/T108 diesel	37'	31.25'	12.5'	5.5'fin	639	16250lb	GRP	Yes
Moody 28	F2010	12/1985 - 6/1987	"		70	Aft cockpit Aux sloop	18bhp Volvo Penta 2002 diesel	27'6"	23'4"	10'	5'fin 3'6"bilge	355	6550lb 6850lb	GRP	Yes
Moody 346	G3010	6/1986 - 7/1990	"		254	Centre cockpit Aux sloop	35bhp/28bhp Thorneycroft T80/90 Volvo Penta 2003 Diesel	34.5'	27'9"	11'8"	5'fin 3'9" bilge	514	11200lb	GRP	Yes
Moody 422	D4010	9/1986 - 6/1988	"		72	Centre cockpit Aux sloop	4cyl 50bhp Thorneycroft diesel	42'	34.25'	13.34'	6'fin 4.66' shoal		21000lb 21780lb	GRP	Yes
Moody Eclipse 33	K1010	12/1987 - 4/1994	"		253	Deck saloon Aux sloop	43/28/29bhp Volvo 2003 Volvo 2003 Turbo Perkins Perama Diesel	32'6"	28'	11'2"	4'9"fin 3'8"bilge	525	12465lb 13000 lb	GRP	Yes
Moody 425	D5010	8/1988 - 7/1991	"		116	Centre cockpit Aux sloop	4cyl 50bhp Thorneycroft Diesel	41.66'	34.25'	13.34'	6'fin 4.66" shoal		21780lb	GRP	Yes
Moody 336	L1010	12/1988 - 6/1995	Bill Dixon	Plymouth	200	Aft cockpit Aux sloop	28bhp/29bhp Volvo 2003 Perkins Perama M30 diesel	33'6"	28'9"	11'7"	5'6"fin 3'11" bilge	478	12584lb	GRP	Yes
Moody Eclipse 43	F3010	12/1989 - 8/1991	"		38	Deck saloon Aux sloop	4cyl 78bhp Perkins M8OT Diesel	42.5'	36.8	14'	4.83'		23000lb	GRP	Yes
Moody 35	G5010	7/1990 - 4/1996	"		192	Centre cockpit Aux sloop	35/34/39bhp Thorneycroft T80 Perkins Perama Volvo Penta 2040 Diesel	34'6"	28'10"	11'11"	5'3"fin 3'11" bilge	505	12800lb 13300lb	GRP	Yes
Moody Eclipse 38	B5010	12/1990 - 2/2992	"		24	Deck saloon Aux sloop	4cyl 59bhp Perkins M60 diesel	37'6"	32'3"	13'	4'6"	777	16250lb	GRP	Yes
Moody 44	D6010	8/1991 - 9/1996	"		114	Centre Cockpit Aux sloop	4cyl 50bhp Perkins Prima M50 Volvo Penta MD22L Diesel	44'	36'	13'8"	6'6"fin 4'11" shoal	994	23000lb 23631lb	GRP	Yes
Moody 38	C9010	9/1991 - 4/1996	"		163	Centre cockpit Aux sloop	3/4cyl 34/50bhp Perkins Perama M35 Perkins PerimaM50 Volvo MD22L Diesel	37'6"	31'6"	12'8"	5'9"fin 4.6" shoal	740	18000lb	GRP	Yes
Moody S31	E3010	5/1994 - 2/1998	"		145	Aft cockpit Aux sloop	19bhp VolvoPenta2020 Diesel	31'9"	26'6"	10'10"	5'6"fin 3'9"bilge	385	10617lb	GRP	Yes

Model type	Yard No From	Build duration	Designer	Place built	No. Built	Type	Engine	LOA	LWL	Beam	Draft	Sail area sq ft	Displ	Material	Photo
Moody S38	B4010	10/1995 - 6/1998	"	"	60	Aft cockpit	40bhp	39'	32'6"	12'11"	6'3"fin	798	19064lb	GRP	Yes
						Aux sloop	VolvoPentaMD2040				4'11"				
							Diesel				shoal				
Moody 36	G6010	7/1996 - 9/2000	"	"	118	Centre cockpit	40bhp	36'9"	30'4"	12'3"	5'9"fin	489	18500lb	GRP	Yes
						Aux sloop	VolvoPentaMD2040				3'11"				
							diesel				bilge				
Moody 40	C1010	12/1996 - 12/1998	"	"	40	Centre cockpit	4cyl 50bhp	40'2"	33'8"	13'3"	6'1"fin	828	23597lb	GRP	Yes
						Aux sloop	VolvoPentaMD22L				4'11"				
							Diesel				shoal				
Moody 46	D7010	12/1997 - 4/2001	"	"	55	Centre cockpit	4cyl 78bhp/75bhp	46'2"	39'4"	14'5"	6'9"fin	1216	31878lb	GRP	Yes
						Aux cutter	Volvo Penta TMD22				5'3"				
						Raised saloon	Yanmar4JH2HTE				shoal		32714lb		
Moody 42	C2010	8/1999 - 3/2002	"	"	55	Centre cockpit	4cyl 50bhp	42'2"	34'10"	13'3"	6'1"fin	823	23641lb	GRP	Yes
						Aux sloop	Volvo Penta MD22L				4'11"				
							Diesel				shoal				
Moody 54	J3010	3/2000 -12/2004	Bill Dixon	Plymouth	55	Raised saloon	4cyl turbo 100bhp	54'11"	46'1"	15'11"	7'6"fin	1693	44132lb	GRP	Yes
						Centre cockpit	Yanmar4JH2-UT				5'11"				
						Aux Cutter	Diesel				shoal				
Moody 38		4/2001 - 2/2003	"	"	37	Centre cockpit	56bhp	37'6"	32'1"	12'4"	6'3"fin	662	18352lb	GRP	Yes
						Aux sloop	Yanmar4JH3				4'9"				
							Diesel				shoal				
Moody 47		5/2001 - 3/2005	"	"	46	Raised saloon	4cyl 78bhp	46'6"	39'5"	14'5"	6'9"fin	1216	32890lb	GRP	Yes
						Centre cockpit	Yanmar4JH3				5'3"				
						Aux cutter	Diesel				shoal				
Moody 64	A1010	6/2003 - 1/2005	"	"	14	Raised saloon	4cyl 230bhp	63'5"	54'3"	17'6"	8'6"fin	1794	33726lb	GRP	Yes
						Centre Cockpit	Yanmar4LHA-STE				6'6"		69080lb		
						Aux Cutter	Diesel				shoal				
Moody 56	J4010	1/2004 - 6/2005	"	"	3	Raised saloon	4cylTurbo100bhp	56'11"	46'2"	15'11"	7'6"fin	1693	44132lb	GRP	Yes
						Centre cockpit	Yanmar4JH2-UT				5'11"				
						Aux Cutter	Diesel				shoal				

Moody Yachts Built by Prout Catamarans Ltd for AH Moody and Son Ltd

Model Type	Yard No	Designer	Place Built	No Built	Type	Engine	LOA	LWL	Beam	Draft	Sail Area	Displ	Material	Photo
Moody Yachts built by Prout Catamarans Ltd for Moody 1999 - 2001														
Moody Excel 31	1999 - 2001	Bill Dixon	Canvey Island	5	Aft cockpit	19bhp	31'9"	26'6"	10'10"	5'6"fin	525	10128lb	GRP	yes
					Aux sloop	VolvoPenta S Drive				3'9"bilge		10617lb		
						MD2020 diesel								
Moody Excel 34	1999 - 2001	"	"	4	Centre cockpit	29bhp	34'	29.20'	11.51'	5.58'fin	514	12786lb	GRP	yes
					Aux sloop	VolvoPenta S drive				3.87'		13331lb		
						MD2030 Diesel				bilge				

Model Type	Build duration	Designer	Place built	No. built	Type	Engine	LOA	LWL	Beam	Draft	Sail Area	Displ	Material	Photo
Moody yachts jointly developed and built by V.T. Halmatic Ltd. Sold and marketed by Moody 2004 - 2005														
Moody 49	2004 - 12/2005	Bill Dixon	Portchester	5	Raised saloon	4cyl 100bhp	48'7"	40'7"	14'5"	6'7"fin	1154	34556lb	GRP	yes
					Centre cockpit	Yanmar4JH3-HTE				5'3" shoal				
					Aux sloop	Diesel								
Moody 56	2004 - 12/2005	Bill Dixon	Portchester	0	Raised saloon	4cyl Turbo100bhp	56'11"	46'2"	15'11"	7'6"fin	1693	44132lb	GRP	yes
					Centre cockpit	Yanmar4JH2-UT				5'11" shoal				
					Aux sloop	Diesel								
Moody 66	2005 - 12/2005	Bill Dixon	Portchester	1	Raised saloon	4cyl 230bhp	65'9"	54'3"	17'6"	8'6"fin	1794	69080lb	GRP	yes
					Centre cockpit	Yanmar4LHA-STE				6'6" shoal				
					Aux sloop	Diesel								